Dandelions of Key West

A Collection of Whimsical Short Stories by Two Military Brats Who Bloomed Within the Conch Community They Now Call Home

Diane Wheeler & Mike Kohut

outskirts
press

Dedication

Our book is dedicated to the children of military families who grew up in different cities, attended many different schools and continually said goodbye to friends as their parents were repeatedly relocated by military orders. Just like Dandelions, they learned to survive and grow under a variety of challenging conditions and environments.

Please visit us at
KeyWestNavyBrats.com

Table of Contents

Preface

O pen this time capsule and discover Key West, Florida through the memoirs of two "Military Brats". These whimsical coming of age stories turn back time to the Key West they knew while growing up as teenagers in the latter half of the 1950s and the first half of the 1960s.

Mike and Diane grew up with Navy Blue & Gold woven into their lives and connected by their shared experience as "Dandelions", the designated flower for military children. Their stories provide a unique perspective and celebrate the resilience of the Dandelion, as well as its ability to thrive and blossom wherever planted. As "Navy Brats", the children of re-assigned career Navy parents, they endured many family moves throughout their gypsy-like childhoods before they were suddenly transplanted into a pristine tropical paradise.

Their short stories recreate the Key West the authors knew, allowing you to experience what it was like to land in the Keys when life was slow paced, the ocean was crystal clear, shrimpers and sailors populated Duval Street and something uniquely spectacular happened almost every day. It was in this setting they fell in love with the Keys and were welcomed into the charming and protective Conch Community of Key West.

They lived their adolescent years on Cayo Hueso (Bone Key) that was brimming with colorful characters, delightful fragrances, and long-lasting friendships. The vast surrounding ocean, azure blue skies and unforgettable sunsets reached out and pointed the way to endless adventures. They each fell in and out of teenage love, tested the limits of their youthful energy and became hopelessly addicted to the alluring adventures of snorkeling and exploring the outer Keys where pirates and buccaneers once roamed. Their tales flash back into early childhood and forward into adulthood so you can better understand the scope and impact of their Key West experience.

 i

The spark for this book began with a stroke of serendipity. In 2003, Diane entered and won a writing contest for a special "Class Ring" story. She had been denied receiving her Key West High School ring when her family was uprooted once again during her senior year. Fifty years later, a friend from Key West fulfilled her dream and presented Diane with her Class Ring. Diane's story was published in the *Palm Beach Post* and eventually reposted in an Internet Group: 'Conch Chatter' run by Ruthie Watler Rivera. This group provided a means where Key West Conchs and Military Brats were able to reconnect, reunite with friends and swap stories.

Like Diane, Mike could not let go of the spell cast by the Keys and began writing short stories about his life in paradise. Through Conch Chatter, these two story tellers were able to connect and plant the seeds of this book. They decided to collaborate and pen the stories of their years in Key West as Navy Brats. Their stories fill a wide canvas with the soft pastel brush strokes of a shy girl and the contrasting colors of wide-eye boy as they paint towards adulthood.

As you read the tales of their escapades, you too will begin to realize how special Key West was and why it continues to draw them back. Although they no longer live in the Keys, it is still considered home. Some call them "Fresh Water Conchs" since they were not born in Key West, but that title does not do justice to the sense of belonging that is felt in their hearts.

Why not bake a batch of Mike's "Chewy Louie ♥ Heart Healthy Cookies" to enjoy while reading their stories? Mike named his cookies after a Key West motorcycle cop for reasons he can't explain. Mike said, "The name just felt right!"

(See Recipes in the Table of Contents)

Maps
(Florida Keys & Key West Dive Map)

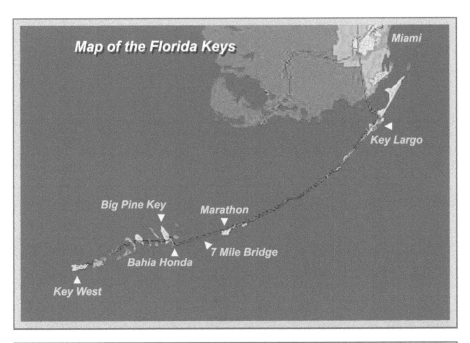

Map of the Florida Keys

Miami

Key Largo

Big Pine Key

Marathon

7 Mile Bridge

Bahia Honda

Key West

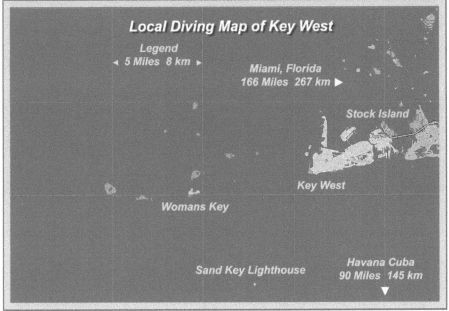

Local Diving Map of Key West

Legend
◄ 5 Miles 8 km ►

Miami, Florida
166 Miles 267 km ►

Stock Island

Key West

Womans Key

Sand Key Lighthouse

Havana Cuba
90 Miles 145 km

1

The Cayo Hueso Blues

Melody based on The John "B" Sails, a traditional Bahamian Folk Song
Music Arrangement by Michael L. Kohut   New Lyrics by Michael & Kathryn Kohut

SETS. CALL FOR THE CAP - TIN A-SHORE, I WAN - A GO HOME. PLEASE LET ME GO
WELLS.STRAN-DED THE CAP - TIN A-SHORE, AND HEAD-ED FOR HOME. JUST GOT TO GET
SHELL. LANDCRABS WEL-COMED US A-SHORE, AND IT FELT LIKE HOME. WE FOUNE A NEW

HOME. CAY-O HUE-SO MY HOME. WELL I, FEEL SO BREAK UP, I
HOME.
HOME.

JUST WANT TO GO HOME. WELL,
I'M,

The Cayo Hueso Blues, Page 2

Lyrics Explained

When people speak about Key West Conchs, they could be referring to a large sea snail that lives in the Gulf of Mexico surrounding the Florida Keys. But, most often the term refers to Key West natives and the long-time residents of Key West.

Americans loyal to the British crown after the Revolutionary War were not very popular, so they fled the southern states to the closest British colony, the town of Spanish Wells in the Bahamas. Unfortunately, the British Parliament started taxing the Bahamians on their food just like they taxed Bostonians on their tea. The Bahamians said they'd rather eat Conch than pay taxes and that is just what they did. They came up with 27 different ways to eat that sea snail. In the 1800s, some of these Bahamian Conchs fled the Bahamas and established new homes in the Florida Keys and Key West.

Throughout the years, many came to know and use the term Conch to describe local residents. Those who made the island their home were proud to be nicknamed Key West Conchs.

To this day, if you are born in Key West you are a "Conch". If you were born elsewhere, but made Key West your home, you are considered a "Fresh Water Conch". Any Conch title is highly revered and worn with pride!

Many famous authors, writers and musicians made Key West their home, or at least a "second home". Especially, Ernest Hemingway, Tennessee Williams and Jimmy Buffet who are also mentioned in Mike's song: "The Cayo Hueso Blues". Cayo Hueso is translated from Spanish as "Bone Key".

Diane's Memoirs & Adventures

Memoirs of a Dandelion
By Diane

I am a dandelion.

A dandelion is a sunny, yellow flower that has the ability to send its feathery seeds sailing in the air at the whim of the breeze that discovers them. In flight, the dandelion's gossamer seeds are light and delicate, but the roots and the yellow blooms are strong and resilient. Besides being known as a pesky yard flower, a dandelion has also become the designated flower of military "brats." This band of gypsy children is frequently scattered far and wide; our lives filled with new schools, brief friendships and unfamiliar surroundings. It is a life of mobility, filled with teary goodbyes and an acquired taste for new beginnings. One could say that the string of orders that carries our families across the globe also develops an innate ability to bloom wherever we are planted. Thus, it was my destiny to be a dandelion.

My journey as a dandelion began on a steamy summer June day decades ago when I came into the world at a Navy hospital in Warrington, Florida. My dad was in flight training at Pensacola, Florida. My mother told me it was 103°F (39°C) the day I decided to make my grand entrance. She was a Midwestern girl and did not take easily to the steamy Florida heat. To be fair, back in those days there was no air conditioning and the muggy room where I was born had a single open window with a small fan blowing on us. I was destined to become the "Queen of the Summer Girls," embracing the sultry summer days in Florida, and my mom clings to the horrific tale of giving birth in sweltering heat!

Thus began the gypsy life of a military brat and an authentic Florida gal. I lived in a string of places after that. I have never officially visited the place I was born, only whizzing past Pensacola on Interstate 10. My first vivid memories of childhood began when I lived near the end of a runway in Norfolk, Virginia. Right by my bedroom window was a huge gardenia bush and on summer nights, the scent of gardenia would fill every corner of my room with its fragrance. To this day, I love gardenias. Then, we moved to Memphis, where we lived on Spring Lake and I learned the merits of fishing with a bamboo pole, watching tadpoles change into tiny frogs, pulling pet ducks in my red wagon, and acquiring a never-ending case of poison ivy. Funny how those early years contribute to what we love as adults--with the exception of poison ivy, of course. We had several more stops before my father got orders back to Florida.

Although Christmas was getting close, we packed our lives up once again into stacks of cardboard boxes and headed to our new home in Jacksonville, Florida. Even in those days Jacksonville was a large, sprawling city with coconut palms and stately oak trees, dripping with Spanish moss. When we first arrived on Christmas Eve, we stayed in a two- story, white, wood-framed Southern guest house with pillars on the veranda and a big winding staircase just inside the door. At the foot of the stairs stood a dazzling Christmas tree. I was the only guest under the age of twenty-five that night but took a chance and left a letter for Santa—fairly concerned that he would be unable to locate me on such sudden notice, no matter how well behaved I had been, in a brand new state. In the morning I discovered a baby doll and some Golden books. I was relieved Santa was aware of my relocation in Florida. I was a Florida girl anyway and it became clear to me that I truly belonged in Florida, leaving me optimistic about my new home.

I attended first grade in Jacksonville. Those were very happy days for me. I walked to and from school with the three neighbor girls—Suzanne, Julianne and Leonie. They had wild, curly hair and syrupy sweet accents.

Their parents let them play outside barefoot. Not mine. On the way home from school, we always stopped off to buy a cup of plain ice for the steamy walk home. I felt very independent and grown up being allowed to walk home on city streets and carry pennies for ice. I am not really sure if I liked school all that much, although I did enjoy coloring with my own personal stash of crayons that were tucked into an authentic cigar box, which still held the lingering scent of tobacco. That year I drank from the Fountain of Youth, visited the Castillo de San Marcos, and studied the arrival of Ponce de Leon and the subsequent battles with native tribes. Even at this tender age, places such as Micanopy and Ichetucknee Springs rolled off my tongue. Chief Osceola became my hero. I was a true Floridian in training.

As a baby boomer, my classes were filled to the brim with students and I was a quiet girl. I counted 40 first graders in my school picture. I miraculously picked up a little reading and math. I acquired a little southern drawl and that still slips into my speech now and then. I loved beach trips with my mom and dad and remember playing in the breakers at St. Augustine beach. I have always been at home in the ocean—diving in and out of the curling waves and gathering shells along the shore. I took the occasional jelly fish stings and encounters with sea creatures in my stride. I still love to body surf in the breakers and suspect those of us born in Florida may have a touch of mermaid in our family tree. In nearby St. Augustine all the little Spanish girls had pierced ears and I wanted them with all my being from the first instant I saw them. They seemed very exotic and grownup looking. For a little girl that still believed in Santa and the Tooth Fairy, as well as the Easter Bunny, it was a long, wistful wait until I was almost out of high school for my wish to finally be realized. This is what happens when you inherit parents from the Midwest and you are a Florida girl. They were in no hurry for me to grow up.

At the end of first grade, we once again loaded up the cardboard boxes and set out to Virginia. It would be seven years before I would cross that Florida line again. I spent the rest of my elementary school years packing and unpacking boxes from Norfolk to Annapolis and even farther north to Rhode Island for junior high. At the end of junior high, my dad got orders to the Fleet Sonar School in Key West, Florida. I had never really heard of Key West, a tiny unknown dot on a map. We began our journey down the east coast to the southernmost part of the United States. I do not think either of my parents were very happy about this tour of duty because at that time it was a step off the beaten path and inconvenient. I do not think I had much sympathy for their "practical" problem because I was so wrapped up in the midst of my own personal teenage tragedy. I had just left behind a flock of girlfriends once again.

I spent the entire trip to Florida, teary-eyed about my plight in life. The gypsy life gets harder as you get older. True, by the time I was fourteen, I had a lot of sad goodbyes under my belt. I had a red plastic transistor radio pressed up against the window listening to the blend of static and music and was prepared for a long, painfully slow trip that was to take me hundreds of miles from my friends. It was August and the temperature was sweltering and humid. Little did I imagine, as our family crept south in our white Plymouth sedan towards our destination in Key West that the breezes were carrying me to a place where my heart would put down roots just like a dandelion. It is the landing that solidified and created the flip-flop wearing Florida gal that I will always be.

Note:

The stories I have written were inspired by my years growing up in Key West. Like my co-author, Mike, I felt as if the Keys were my first real home. After reading his adventurous memories, I realize I did not take "full" advantage of the trouble and fun I might have found. I was a lot more timid and my parents had me on a much tighter leash. If I had those years to live over, I would have wished to cross paths with Mike so I could have expanded my horizons a bit!

I wrote my stories based on how I recall feeling in the moment, so I would like to say that I may sound a bit hard on my parents. Somehow I have actually become much wiser. Now I have two daughters that survived my parenting with mixed reviews. The handbook that comes with parenthood is written in tiny unintelligible print. The path is not straight and sometimes pretty rocky.

I can only imagine how challenging it must have been to be uprooted so frequently and to rebuild a home in new surroundings. My father's career in the military trumped every other family choice. It is a life of great commitment and often sacrifice. My mom was a wonderful role model of resilience and had to forfeit her own career and education until much later in life, due to the constant relocations. She persisted until she finally received her degree. My father was frequently gone and life went on. (This was great preparation for my years as a single parent. I already knew it could be done.) And, as you will see I was sort of an "alien" child raised in a completely different environment than my parents. It must have been quite a challenge for them.

In retrospect, I do not at all "blame" my parents for our unsettled life. I have treasured and nurtured my old friendships, especially those from the Keys. I have many good friends that reach back to early years. I like being a dandelion. While I mourned lost friendships, now I also celebrate the richness of the big wide world I grew up in filled with new places and people. I am comfortable with unknowns in life and have been credited with being a free spirit. After all, the one constant in life is change.

Misplaced Mermaid Finds a Home
By Diane

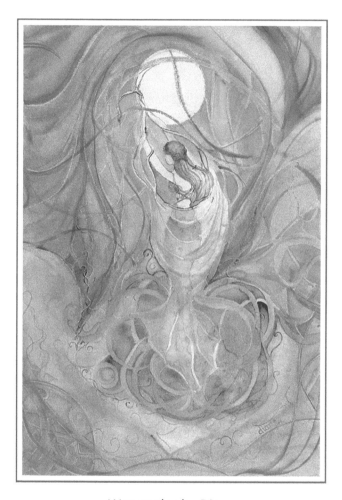

Watercolor by Diane
Mermaid in Moonlight

For some reason, quite naturally, when children enter that passage-way to adolescence, children and parents can become potential ad-versaries. My parents had very high expectations for my path in life and they ran a *tight ship* as they say in the Navy. What I was feeling in that moment was pain from yet another separation from friends which had already left me "angsty" and somewhat moody. My one and only best friend was moving to Virginia and I was moving to an unknown blip on the map called Key West. As we continued our journey towards the next tour of duty in the Keys, I spent my melancholy hours listening to music in the backseat of the car and began building a solid case for my emancipation from this life filled with goodbyes.

For one thing, I felt my parents were uniquely unqualified to advise me on how to survive my life. Both of my parents grew up in small towns in Illinois, surrounded by family and friends. We visited Illinois often enough for me to know that their lives were decidedly different from my own gypsy life. Besides cornfields and farms, it was also home to brick streets, porch swings, Sunday fried chicken dinners with family, and stores filled with people everyone knew. The children hatched in those small towns entered first grade with the same friends and classmates they walked down the aisle with at their graduations. Yet, my parents were still clinging to the idea that I would grow up on the same path as they did. This was a note of optimism on their part. All of my wanderings had opened up windows to the big, wide world and I knew there was more than one highway in life. In that moment, I did not know that A1A would take me to the place I call home.

It was a long drive through Florida in those days. Many of the highways were still two-lane and wound through sleepy Florida towns with speed traps and cafes with ceiling fans and screen doors. When we got through Miami into Homestead, there was an abrupt turn that seemed to be the end of the line by a sugar cane field. Although it seemed like we had reached the end of the road, I was wrong. It was the beginning of a highway that was to change the course of my life forever. We drove on a narrow state highway taking us through the brackish wetlands and the bridges that lead to Key Largo. From the moment I saw the Florida Keys, my view of the world began to change. Narrow, two-lane bridges connected the islands. There was barely room for two cars to meet on the bridges and it was a slow journey through the upper keys. When your dad can land a plane on an aircraft carrier, you do not really worry much about driving on the bridges. Those were the days when the narrow bridges turned away many tourists who retreated quickly back to the mainland.

When we reached the middle keys, the sky and water filled the horizon—a myriad of crystal clear blues and greens. Low drifting stacks of cumulus clouds floated across the sky. The brilliant orange colors of the Poinciana trees dotted the lush landscape of palms and tropical green plants. Even in the *dog days* of summer, it clearly was the most beautiful place I had ever seen—and I had seen a lot of places! The air was sultry and there were little "Old Florida" one story motels shaded by palm trees. They were typically pastel pink or aqua concrete structures with matching concrete tables with sun-faded umbrellas and benches too hot to sit on. There was usually a little pier and a few boats would be tied up in the slips. Tucked in between the motel and dock you could normally find a tiny, shallow sandy beach created for ocean-wading, the kind you drag your lounge chair into to stay cool. Even a pool was a luxury in those days.

At 14 years old, I had the wisdom to see the possibility that the Keys would be great place for a gypsy girl—born in Florida with wildly romantic notions about life—part mermaid, who carried the hope of pierced ears, sea breeze on my face and perhaps a gardenia pinned behind my ear? The journey down the Keys took about three hours even without parades of traffic you find nowadays. Although my parents may have been trying to resign themselves to the impractical fate of this tour of duty, I had become secretly revenged for this recent uprooting by the love I felt for new home. This was going to be a great adventure in life. I could feel it

Key West, 1961... Those who were lucky enough to know what it was like in Key West in 1961 can imagine what I thought as I crossed that last little bridge into Key West. It was filled with colors, sounds and salt-water smells and it took my breath away. It is actually an amazing thing to be a military brat. Sometimes it was lonely, even more so for me as I was an only child. Your home is ever-changing. You make a home where you are planted. You recreate your life again and again. To this day, I usually hang up my family pictures and artwork first, making the new place seem like an instant home. You become adept at switching gears and reinventing your life on a moment's notice. Life is filled with unknowns—never knowing who or what awaits around the bend in the road.

Home could be military quarters, gray from wall to wall—on a Navy base guarded by Marines at the gate. There, as drab as it may have been, it was easy to find commonality with other military families and life was usually filled with instant friendships. Or, you could live in a far more visually-appealing neighborhood with settled, tree-lined streets, facing the challenges with being the only new kid on the block. I had already had many homes, found and lost a lot of friends, been the new kid at many schools, adjusted to living in many different climates, and seen many strange towns change into familiar surroundings with time. But, this was a side of my old friend, Florida, that I never knew existed.

Just like the Jimmy Buffett song, *First Look,* my head was dancing, ecstatic with joy, filled with postcard images that had suddenly become real. I am after all, a Florida gal and Key West has it all packed into a tiny little island—old wooden houses with gingerbread cutouts peeking from behind thick tropical trees, narrow bustling streets, ocean breezes with sky and water at the end of almost every street. It suited my free spirit very well and I claimed it as my home in an instant. I think fate arranged for the little girl with gypsy notions to be placed in exactly the perfect spot on earth. And, first love it was! I carry the Keys in spirit no matter where I land in life and have tried to adjust to the compromise of not being able to spend all the days of my life in the spot I claimed as home.

It took a while for us to settle into Key West. We lived in a little motel with a tropical courtyard. The only television was located on the patio and if you wished to watch this lone set, you had to join other residents (mostly older) for the evening and cool off under the ceiling fan. The jalousie windows were always open and the sounds from Key West drifted in until late hours of the night. Hibiscus bloomed outside the little cottage and tiny geckos hung silently from awnings and walls. The nights in Key West are balmy and stars and moon are suspended brightly overhead. Gentle breezes blow from the ocean. It is no wonder Tennessee Williams chose to live and write there because he was also clearly as smitten by the steamy southern nights as I was. This was the backdrop for much of his work. Now and then we would see him on this little island that we shared with many artists.

In this setting, I began my high school years. They were filled with a collection of much-loved friends, first love, first kiss, high school dances and football games plus a touch of algebra, Latin, chemistry, and stacks of classic required literature. Although the climate wiped out any hope of smooth hair, I spent most of my time outdoors swimming, biking and snorkeling. I set my frizzy hair with orange juice cans in an effort to tame the effects of the humidity, but it did not work. With love, you must accept the downside. I took painting lessons at Martello Towers from an artist who lived on houseboat row. I developed a passion for key lime pie, brown bags of conch fritters, and *café con leche*. We all wore penny loafers (with no socks and blisters), bleeding madras and of course, skimpy bikinis. It is Florida after all.

In the true spirit of an emancipated teenager, I battled my parents over short skirts, teased hair, white lipstick and black eyeliner. (In retrospect, my parents may have been right about the teased hair and white lipstick!) All of these were mostly in the "nixed" category of the pierced ears that I still longed for. But, my heart had found roots in Key West and I had claimed it as my home. Although I would never qualify as a Conch and I would eventually move far away, no other place would ever really take that trophy. I had found the home I had always longed to have.

Academic Doldrums
By Diane

The doldrums, by definition, is a region near the equator of inactivity that is prone to sudden storms. My parents had determined a very lofty academic path for me. My father literally was a math and engineering genius. Math assistance in our home was not unlike the movie *Good Will Hunting* with yellow legal pads covered with uninterpretable math. In case you never watched this movie, it involves math genius and a blackboard filled with unsolved equations, which look foreign to the average person. My mother was a motivated honor student. Although in Rhode Island I was placed in the highest ranked class out of thirteen groups, I always felt there had been an error. I was a daydreamer who drew endless pictures down the margins of my papers as the teachers' voices droned on. I believe that my trek for the top was probably always doomed.

Upon my arrival in Key West, far closer to the equator, my scholarly decline began to take on some real momentum. I was, of course, in college-bound programs and planned to attend a university someday. However,

Key West was so filled with color, life, sounds, and endless distraction not academic in any way. The tropics threw me into a new state of mind immediately.

This decline began with a slightly late start my freshman year. Suddenly Mr. Simpson's geometry class sounded like a foreign language. My first truly botched assignment was a bug collection for Mr. Marzyck's biology class. Now, anyone who has visited Florida knows that it is a world class bug-collecting spot. Its bugs are bigger and creepier than anywhere else in the good old U.S.A. Anyone who has met one of the colossal palmetto bugs realizes there are endless opportunities to gather amazing specimens. Although I was new in school and one would have thought that I would have wanted to place my best foot forward. Not so.

Thankfully my father was attempting to return his vehicle to pristine condition after our long drive. His efforts inspired me with an easy solution to my problem as our radiator grill was loaded with ill-fated insects. This became my prime source for my insect collection. My rather-serious and dry biology teacher did not even wince when I submitted my beautifully-labelled insect collection displaying mangled insects that were missing random wings and extremities. It was a sensational beginning to my beginning of the less-effort/marginal-reward approach to high school.

My one bright spot was Latin. The teacher, Vera Walden was very eccentric. She wore black cat eye glasses with rhinestones before they were "in." They actually seemed to approach bat wing glasses. For some unknown reason Latin was sort of a useless strong suit for me. She also sponsored a Latin Club. Lost academic soul that I had by now become, for some reason, I loved that club. First year students were purchased in an unfortunate reenactment of a slave auction. Second year students became masters and if you continued to strive, you could become a Roman god or goddess. Becoming a goddess was indeed a lofty goal.

We had a rather G-rated toga party and banquet which included a slave auction. By a stroke of luck, I was purchased by a cute guy named John Eller with dimples and dreamy eyes. My best friend was in love with him and was thrilled with my slave status. It was the highlight of our day if he asked me to carry his tray to clear it off after lunch. This alone shows how misguided my direction was at this point. We devised a tactic to get his attention that equaled Caesar's campaign on Britannia. Our plan was to casually stroll past his house, which was completely across the island from home as many times as possible in a week. So the two of us who complained incessantly about having to run the track in P.E. walked all the way to White Street for a glimpse of his house. In other words, we were teenage stalkers. We had become two desperate teenage girls on a quest. Our campaign was pretty successful at appearing casual because fifty years later, I discovered he had NO idea about the efforts we were taking to be noticed. In fact, he barely knew who we were.

In the meantime, I had fallen deeply in "love" with Brian, a student who worked in Gallagher Music Store for his brother Gene, who played in a popular local band. It was a sort of claim to fame (at that low point in our lives) if they even spoke to us. I had zero dollars for records but we added that stop to our rather athletic circuit. This was yet another distraction for me from school work. I decorated my book covers with his name in a "subtle" effort to win his heart. I am not sure if it was my artistic rendering of his name or my frequent music store visits, but one day he asked for my phone number. Then he called me. Much to my parents' dismay, Brian became my steady boyfriend. I spent all of my time on the phone and writing notes. I could have written a novel with the same amount of energy.

"Love" had now derailed any hope of good grades. My aspiration was to get good enough grades so that I would not be grounded for the rest of high school. This led to my biggest debacle, which was a science fair project for Mr. Lazier's chemistry class. Although, I recall he was an excellent teacher, I fell short in Chemistry. As mentioned before, science and math were my father's genius, not mine. I was uniquely unmotivated. However, we made a special trip to Coral Gables to a hobby shop to purchase samples of different types of metals for a project on oxidation. I believe once again my father's vehicle was the inspiration for this project. He felt the tropical heat and salt air were waging war on his mufflers and was pretty much perpetually annoyed with having to replace them. So while my father was concerned with rusty tailpipes, I was in "love" and nothing else really mattered.

Rule number one for a study of oxidation: Do not procrastinate. My father was wrong about the speed with which things rusted in Key West. I waited until the last minute to begin my project. This left me with only one conclusion—no metals rust in salt water. In fact, oxidation is non-existent. This was a newsworthy scientific outcome. It was especially disconcerting to my father who had both inspired me and taken me to Miami to get the materials. Making all of this far worse, my neighbor and minister's daughter had an absolutely spectacular project. I did not comprehend what her project was, nor do I now. But as we wandered through the gym filled with science fair projects, my father looked wistfully at Junior's (my neighbor's nickname) project: The Determination of the Decomposition of Amino Acids using Paper–Electrophoresis. Unfortunately, my botched project was also on display. I am sure I received an effort grade that exceeded my actual effort. The demise of my academic journey was at an all-time high. My father became rather quiet as his "tight ship" was sinking rapidly.

I noticed my plan towards emancipation was working. I was finally allowed to go to the drive-in. I think my mom bought me more mature clothes and a sort of conservative version of a bikini. Still, no pierced ears were in the cards. My hair continued to frizz and curl relentlessly but life was good. I was going steady but my school work was careening towards the rocks. We should treasure and fondly recall those intense feelings of our youth. They were the beginnings of the wiser adult that eventually emerges—the seeds of the flower that blooms.

Fortunately, because my family and teachers believed in me during those uncertain and tumultuous years, I found my niche in life. I became inspired to want to change the world, one child at a time. I earned my BS degree at Illinois State University and a Master's degree in Multicultural Education from Florida Atlantic University. I was able to enjoy 30 rich years of teaching. Ironically, I organized science fairs, though I still doodle on my papers.

Missiles in Paradise
By Diane

Sketch book of Memories

*U*pon reflection, it seems that besides the usual turmoil of teen years, the biggest change experienced is the ability to recognize human struggles beyond your own adolescent realm. In 1959 Fidel Castro became the dictator in Cuba. Upon my arrival in Key West, I witnessed the miraculous arrivals of many refugees fleeing Cuba. They arrived on boats and other pieced-together ingenious floating rafts, brimming with courageous people who had survived the 90-mile (145 km) trek across the Straits of Florida to American soil.

Although I was immersed in more trivial teenage matters such as hair, romance and school work (in that order), the human exodus from Cuba did not go unnoticed. The boats and salvage littered the waterways and beaches around Key West and were a reminder that there was a much larger world beyond my own cocoon.

In October of 1962, a U-2 spy plane took photos revealing Soviet ballistic missiles located in Cuba, a serious threat to our country. Somewhere between football games and school dances, I became aware we were in imminent danger. For most of the United States, this event was not quite the same as it was for those of us living in the Keys. We experienced this moment from a very close proximity and a unique perspective.

Our family listened to President John F. Kennedy on the radio in our darkened living room. Mind you, we had a television in our Florida room but my father refused to pay for cable. He believed pay television was gouging him and further justified this decision saying this gave me more time for study and less time in front of the "idiot" box. Therefore we only had local channels that scrolled weather across the screen and occasionally on a good atmospheric day, we could pick up a Cuban channel. So, although we lived in the fanciest house we had ever lived in on Riviera Drive, our family had listened in silence on the radio to the announcement that Russian missiles had been found in Cuba and that our Navy was forming a military blockade to stop the Soviet ships bound for Cuba, a mere 90 miles away from Key West.

My father had spent almost the entirety of his military career submarine hunting. He had been in anti-submarine warfare squadrons that mostly were focused on cat-and-mouse games with Soviet subs. In Key West, he was assigned to the Fleet Sonar School. He did not appear surprised by the military action our country was taking. Any concern he may have had was handled with the absolute calm any military officer should have demonstrated. We had observed the buildup of air traffic in the Keys for several days, creating a slow rise in concern and accentuating the great uncertainty of this cold war era. What we did not know was whether the Soviet ships would turn or continue, possibly triggering a nuclear attack. Many predicted it could be the beginning of the end of days. These were sobering headlines—even for a teenager with only fifteen years of experience in life. We were children of the Cold War era though; the threat of nuclear attack was not completely new to us. However, being in Key West, a mere 90 miles away from Cuba did intensify the experience. We watched and waited with great apprehension.

In the dark of night the army entered our little island town, which was accustomed to a strong Navy presence, but not the sound of trucks and tanks rumbling down our streets. Since some of this military traffic came right down Flagler Avenue, just a block from our street, I listened nervously in the dark. In just one night it seemed that Key West was transformed into a militarized zone. Barbed wire with armed soldiers lined the city and county beaches. Anti-aircraft rockets were pointed out at the Straits of Florida. The beautiful old Casa Marina hotel had become a home for army soldiers. Signs of impending war filled our beautiful island.

From our high school windows, we watched army troops assembling scaffolding for an ominous radar installation. Military planes and helicopters were humming overhead as they guarded our shores. During the next few days many families came to school to pull students from class to evacuate the Keys to homes on the mainland. There were many teary goodbyes with friends we wondered if we would ever see again. As we waited for the Soviet ships to reach our blockade, we all held our breath in fear.

Being a military brat, I knew the gravity of the situation because my father flew many long hours during those weeks. It is very personal when you are that close to the reality of a crisis. At the same time I still saw these events through the eyes of a teenager, wondering if I was ever going to see those pierced ears I had waited for since first grade. I also wondered if I would live to become the captivating woman I anticipated, rather than remaining the gentle whisper of what I might have become in time. Would I die the awkward and shy teenager who had never truly "lived" yet? We were not the kind of family that panicked and ran. We also did not battle over the last loaves of bread and milk on the grocery shelves. I was, in fact, far more preoccupied with how long I was to be grounded to my house, which could become the entire remainder of what may be a shortened life. My father's response to this crisis was to limit my social life to school and home and I was in a big hurry for resolution of this event. Despite being caught in the web of this crisis, I still continued to view the world through the innocent haze of my youth.

I had a passion for living out my dreams and might have added a few more sophisticated ones during that crisis. I had acquired a desire to change the world and had discovered a sense of urgency to live life fully before those in power managed to cut it short. I did not want to miss a thing in life. I was barely surviving my parents holding me so tightly by the reins and now it seemed like there was an adult conspiracy to possibly end the full bloom of my life before I was even allowed to live it.

On October 28, 1962, the Cuban Missile Crisis passed and life slowly returned to normal after a tense thirteen days. However, I felt a little older after coming to terms with the possibility of my imminent mortality and far more in touch with the world outside the closed circle of teenage life. It was a time of change in the 60s. On November 22nd, during study hall in the auditorium, Capt. Ecklund, holding back tears, informed us that John F. Kennedy had been assassinated in Dallas, Texas. This stunning assassination touched most of us in a very personal way. We cried together, mourning his death. Another piece of our collective innocence was lost that day.

Our generation witnessed many acts of courage and sacrifice by those trying to find equality and create a better way of life in America. We watched the poignant and sometimes violent battle for Civil Rights unfold on television. In 1964 the Civil Rights Act was ratified. During our junior year our high school was integrated. Looking back, I feel somewhat amazed how unaware I was of the full extent of injustices that had been in plain view for most of my life. My parents had not neglected to develop sense of social awareness in me. They were uncomfortable with the "Whites Only" signs we had encountered in our travels and did not fail to discuss the painful evidence of racism we witnessed. However, it was not until this time in my life that I truly began to fathom the deep-rooted prejudice that many faced in life. The hushed voices now had become shouts for equal rights. This change unfolded very peacefully and quietly at our high school. Still, we had become a part of much larger movement that was underway. Over the next few years, we would witness remarkable valor from ordinary people who rose to greatness.

During high school we had been a part of events that brought both fear and loss, but also had sparked a passion for justice and movement for change. In 2012, almost 50 years later, I stood on the steps of the Lincoln Memorial with my students while visiting our nation's capitol on a safety patrol trip. This trip took place during the administration of our first African American president and was during the celebration of Martin Luther King's birthday. Without any prompting, these ten-year-old students huddled in the cold over the plaque tracing and touching the spot that commemorated the delivery of Martin Luther King's "I Have a Dream" speech. Tears rolled down my cheeks as I watched them make an emotional connection with the same history that I had witnessed unfold during my high school years.

Right in the midst of our intense growing up years, the world around us was evolving and we were learning the fragile nature about life. We seemed to have become less safe and less assured of our futures. None of us realized that some of our friends would soon find themselves in Vietnam, many losing their lives in a country half-way around the world. The names of those friends are now etched on a wall, yet we recall them still as young and alive. We listened to the Beatles and the Rolling Stones together and searched for answers in our young lives. We wondered what kind of a world we would be creating when we took the helm.

Snippets in the Sand
By Diane

Sun Washed Angel

All of us know that as the years advance, the sand in the hourglass seems to slip through a lot more rapidly. A few years ago, I traveled back to Key West to celebrate the reunions of the classes of 1965 and

1966. I enjoyed talking to many old classmates and rejoiced in catching up with many old friends. Of course, Conchs call Key West home. However, an astounding number of military brats, like me, call Key West home as well. I wonder if we just actually deserve a special designation beyond "fresh-water Conchs." We only passed through for a short time, but the impact Key West and the friends we made there has lasted a lifetime. We seem to all return time after time to keep these treasured connections.

Good Old Days

Our little island was very different back in the sixties. I liked it when A1A was still a narrow, more daunting highway to drive and it was not so crowded with tourists. It was full of weathered homes that did not have million-dollar mortgages. Tourists stayed mostly in quiet, little "old Florida" motels and quietly celebrated the water and the ocean. We were fortunate to share a truly unique way of life with our Conch classmates and we tirelessly retell our old stories. Upon our arrival, our classmates led the way for many of us as we acclimated and prepared for our new life in paradise.

Scary Stories

One of my fond but chilling memories begins in the cemetery. I visit there every time I return. In fact, Key West has no shortage of ghost stories and hauntings. Walking through the narrow streets with the old wooden homes, the long history of Key West makes it easy to imagine ghostly whispers from the colorful past on this little island. When I was in high school, I took art classes at East Martello Towers, a former Civil War era fort, which has been said to be haunted by the soldiers that died there from yellow fever. I always had one eye on my painting and one on the lookout for ghosts.

One evening during my sophomore year of high school, several of my friends and I were enjoying a sleepover–the kind with no sleep and a lot of talking and some shenanigans. We all went for a walk that passed by the cemetery on this balmy evening. As we walked past the open gate, we came up with a great idea for creepy entertainment.

We devised a game which involved entering the gates on Angela Street and exiting on Frances Street–alone. It was almost nightfall when we began to draw straws to see who would go through first. Our little game of "chicken" began. A few people were ahead of me so by the time it was my turn, a blanket of darkness had descended upon the city. I was already frightened before I even began to walk into the cemetery. This seemed like a theme for a really cheesy scary movie that was destined to run amuck and end badly. Although two of my friends had already returned safely, luck could run out. There was not a doubt in my mind that this beautiful and lonely spot was haunted, hopefully by understanding spirits. As I began my walk down the narrow road and stared into the darkness, I could see shadows dancing between the above-ground graves and behind the mausoleums. I strained my eyes to see in the dark, scanning the cemetery for anything that could be moving or lurking in the shadows waiting to reach out for me.

Somehow, probably due to my less than outstanding sense of direction, I got off course and truly could not be sure where the exit was. I stopped walking and stood in silence, hoping I could regain my wits. As I stood there in the darkness, I heard soft rustling off to one side. It was a moonlit night, yet I could not be sure what I was seeing. As I stood there, I called out to my friends thinking that maybe they were trying to scare me, which seemed very likely. No answer. The faint swishing sound continued and seemed to be creeping closer. As I stood there it felt as if someone was breathing and whispering behind me. The hair stood up on the back of my neck and a chill came over me. I was convinced that someone unseen had brushed by me ever so closely in the darkness. Now I was truly frozen with fear and with no clear path forward I decided to turn around and run the gauntlet back towards Angela Street. I started slowly; then I gained speed and did not look back.

By the time I reached my friends, my heart was racing and tears were running down my face. Although it was a warm night, I still felt icy spots on my neck and arms as if a ghost had touched me. I will never know if I encountered a spirit that night or if my imagination won the battle against logic. I have always hoped ever since that moment that we did not disturb the souls resting there. For a long time, I half expected to be cursed or haunted because of our silly game. I gladly accepted the humble label of "chicken" and considered myself lucky to be back with my friends.

None of my friends had been inside the cemetery that night with me so I concluded that my encounter was with a spirit. This would not be the only encounters I had with the other world in my lifetime. As an adult, I have had several other ghostly experiences that were peaceful in nature. In Lake Worth, Florida, I truly believe I lived in a haunted house. Either I am open to the power of suggestion or, I am just one of those lucky people singled out for "special" visits from the other side.

To this day though, I love actually visiting the Key West cemetery, which is rich in history and generally quite peaceful, with the exception of the tourists who now haunt that spot frequently.

One funny sidebar to this event was that in 1980 when I returned to Key West as a teacher, my daughter came home with a faded pastel wreath that had the word "Mother" inscribed on it. I knew instantly that it had come from the same cemetery. She was so excited with this gift that I hated to tell her we clearly needed to return this plastic floral memorial to the sacred spot it had been removed from. I gathered the little crew of girls and we returned to the scene of the crime. Of course, we were unable to locate the *right* mother, so we left the flowers on a woman's grave there. I did not want to invite any trouble with spirits in a clearly haunted place like Key West.

Dead in the Water

The water was the heart of life in the Keys. If I was not at the Truman Annex pool for endless hours, you could find me on the beach. I had a pair of faded Keds (our version of athletic shoes) with frayed toes that were reserved for walking gingerly past the coral, sea urchins and sharp rocks at the beach. In the sixties, ocean life was abundant and conchs and horseshoe crabs were a frequent discovery. We all swam in harmony with the sea creatures. At night you could see the luminescent ocean life that lit up the current. Our lives were connected to the water, as were many of my escapades.

On yet another slumber party episode, I had a rather unexpected water adventure. My friends and I had plans to take a sailing dinghy from Stock Island, around Sigsbee Point, to a little island beach near Garrison Bight. We were meeting a few friends with a catamaran that morning. We began our little voyage with a bang, when the wind suddenly caught the sail, and the boom flew across hitting me in the nose. I was pretty sure that the nose that I was already somewhat dissatisfied with was broken. Fortunately, it was not, although I certainly learned the meaning of what a "boom" was. I was left with what eventually became a bruise and faint dark circles under my eyes.

Optimistically, we continued on our quest for adventure and a day in the sun! My friend had a little experience sailing and I had quite a lot less than that. We set sail and our voyage seemed pretty easy. There were gentle breezes, just enough to push us through the water but not very challenging to maneuver. Who would have dreamed that any trip so glorious—filled with sun, saltwater and wind—could ever go badly?

We managed to land on the little island beach and enjoyed hours of sailing and socializing on the catamaran, in which time my friend managed to "fall in love." So, when it came time to sail back, she wanted to sail on the catamaran and wanted to know if I could just take the dinghy back alone. After my rather uplifting sailing adventure so far that day, a little reluctantly, I agreed. (My parents would have nixed a sailing trip without adult in the first place and definitely would NOT have felt I was qualified to sail alone. And, they would have been correct.) However, I wanted to be a team player (also known as peer pressure) and I agreed.

It began well as I sailed across Garrison Bight just about until I planned to make the turn along the coast to skirt Sigsbee Park. Then it happened. The wind died. As my friends drifted towards Sigsbee, I started to drift towards Roosevelt Boulevard, a busy thoroughfare. I tried paddling towards my friends. Paddling was clearly not my strong suit and I realized it was useless.

I could tell by the sun it was getting later and I needed to get back before my parents decided to pick me up. So, I dropped the sail and jumped into the water. It was pretty shallow there so I pulled the boat towards

Sigsbee Road. It was a long haul through rocks and seaweed but sadly faster than sailing. Thankfully, I was wearing my worn shoes that day and not barefoot. In a rather bold move that was inspired by desperation, I set my sights on Sigsbee Road as I had decided to carry the boat over the road rather than trying to sail all the way around the point. I prayed my parents or no one that was acquainted with them would see me as it was pretty busy that time of day. I attempted to get the boat up onto the road. That proved to be much harder alone than I anticipated. As I struggled, the Shore Patrol showed up. I thought for sure I was going to be "busted" and my father would have good cause to ground me. However, instead, they helped me carry the boat to the other side of the road. I continued to pray no one familiar would see me.

On the other side of the road, I was able to paddle out and wished for a little breeze. Finally, a faint breeze filled the sail and I was underway again. It was a pretty slow trip back to Stock Island. As I crossed the darker (and deeper) water in a channel, the thought occurred to me that I was pretty much in over my head. It was a bit late in the day for that moment of clarity. I could not really figure out exactly where to return on Stock Island so I landed a bit off target and walked to my friend's house. Her parents were relieved to see me and I was able to explain where the dinghy was and described the dilemma with the dead wind. They picked up the other stranded sailors off Sigsbee (Navy housing) dead in the water and tied up to a buoy. Everyone made it home safely that day. I was relieved and exhausted.

When my mom picked me up, I decided to lie by sin of omission. Our conversation was not the interrogation I had anticipated. Many questions were left unasked. I feel like her urge to know was not quite as big as the fear of knowing the truth about my escapade.

"Did you have fun?"

"Yep," I said.

"What did you do?" I'm sure she observed my generally disheveled state, my windswept hair and the bruising left from my introduction to the boom.

"Oh, we just hung out with some friends," I said, looking down at my sandy, wet tennis shoes.

I am pretty certain she knew there was a story to go with my appearance, but if she knew, she chose to never let on that she suspected a thing. I looked down at my trusty old pair of Keds and redesignated them *lucky, old* Keds. That same old pair of shoes saw me through many joyous days in the sand and water of the Keys. After raising two girls of my own, I am now convinced there is a special set of angels, whose sole job it is to protect teenagers, who are traveling without a lot of common sense through those years.

There's No Place like Home

Living in Key West for high school was a rich adventure, unique to our little island home. I love to recall all the little snippets of my life there in Key West and I feel truly fortunate to have lived there when I did. It has made the reunions sweeter and partings more wrenching. If I could have wished for one place to have grown up, it would have been in the Keys right where I landed. I am looking forward to many more reunions and opportunities to leave my footprints in the sand there.

A toast to all the kids who grew up on our much-loved little island (the Conchs and those of us that landed quite by chance)–*May the sands of time be kind to us all and keep us connected for many years to come.*

Paradise Lost
By Diane

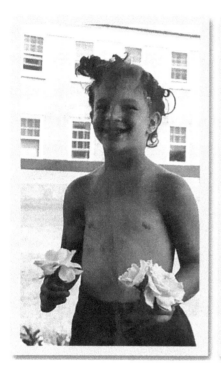 

The power of the gardenia

I was always a quiet, timid and flighty soul that often faded into the background at school. Always the new kid in school almost every single year of my life, I believe being a little invisible was intentional. I spent a great deal of time watching the clouds drift by or listening to the palm trees whispering in the breeze and drawing down the margins of my papers in class.

Despite my transient life, as my junior year began, I had found my niche in Key West. I had large group of friends, mostly other Navy "brats" that congregated at the pool during the summer, watched movies on base for a dime, and they had grown to love living in Key West as much as I did.

My sophomore year had ended in turmoil when my mother had been admitted to the Navy hospital for emergency surgery and found herself fighting for her life. My father, who could land a plane on an aircraft carrier pitching and rolling out at sea at night, did not have even a fundamental understanding of grocery shopping or any other household routines. Since we had no family living nearby, we relied upon the mercy of friends to survive this event. In the nick of time, my sweet and homebody grandmother who lived in rural Illinois mustered up the courage to take her first "new-fangled" plane ride to Key West. This must have been quite a harrowing experience for her as she opted for a very long, arduous train ride back to Illinois. Together, we at least managed to cook some meals and keep the house from total ruin. As my mother was left for more than a month recovering in the hospital, I continued to muddle through high school life. My clothes were wrinkled and our meals were below the usual standard but somehow we managed to function at least at the survival level.

I became much bolder and more independent during that time. I had finished Driver's Education and I am certain that my very nervous teacher, Mr. Butcher, was correct when he made the critique that I was a truly awful driver. My father shared his exasperation with my indecisive and inattentive driving. It no doubt struck fear into them as I tackled the narrow and bustling roads in Key West. Because he had no choice, my father allowed me to drive to the grocery store. These trips were followed by a thorough inspection of every inch of our old white Plymouth (with fins) upon my return. I loved to roll down the windows and turn up the radio and enjoy the glorious feeling of freedom. If I could slip in a few additional minutes, I would swing by a friend's house for a quick chat although I was nervous, convinced my father knew "all."

That summer my parents shipped me off to Blackstone, Virginia to visit close friends. Their daughter, Jesslyn, and I had been long-time friends and had shared two "tours of duty" along our gypsy journey. Our fathers were classmates from Annapolis. I loved living at their home because it was a family of five siblings and they had little time to scrutinize our comings and goings. We even lived in a cute little backhouse with her sister that was not under the same roof as the rest of the family. That summer I smoked my first cigarette, had no real curfew, and as long as the chores were done, we were emancipated kids. When I returned to Key West for my junior year, I was sixteen, a little less sweet, and primed for a bold new life.

Back in Key West, I found that the plan my parents had orchestrated for me diverged from the plan I had been creating as I enjoyed my freedom in Virginia. I bemoaned the fact I could not suddenly find five siblings to take the focus off of my every move. Although I was back home in paradise, there was a downside to the beginning of this year. I knew that my father's assignment at the Fleet Sonar School would end close to the end of the school year and that would probably mean leaving my little island, Key West. I held on to the wish that I could be kidnapped by pirates and held hostage in the Keys. This was my only hope so I would not have to once again be torn from my friends and my home. To be clear, I always had a wonderful house to live in and made friends in all of my many moves—too numerous to count. What I did not always have was a place that was actually home to me. I had claimed Key West and Key West had staked a claim on my very soul. I loved this beautiful placed filled with light, colors, fragrant smells, sky, and sea and dreaded the possibility of having to move from there. Key West was my home now.

As usual, my mother had regained full and efficient control of the household, and was busy creating opportunities for me. She even signed me up for bridge lessons, preparing me to survive life in her fashion. Many Navy brat friends were signed up for these lessons from a Navy wife. These friends and I had to walk there one afternoon a week after school for duplicate bridge. I was disenchanted from the beginning and deemed the walk there with friends to be best part of the lessons! I was even worse at bridge than driving. No doubt this was tortuous for all involved. I tried to finagle my way out of these lessons each week, but generally failed to come up with a good enough excuse. I was convinced there had been a mix-up at the nursery in Pensacola and I had been delivered to the wrong family. This feeling caused my rebellious attitude to bubble over.

My junior year, 1964, was a year marked by the Beatle invasion, Bass Weejuns (without socks), flipped hair styles, and clothes made of "bleeding" madras. I was required to hand wash all of my madras clothes. Anytime I got something made of this plaid I was quickly reminded that it could not go into the washing machine and I was solely responsible for washing those items–the cost of fashion. I began to practice telling my parents what they wanted to hear and pushed the limits as far as humanly possible. That effort was not all that impressive as my father definitely was determined to run a tight ship. There were strict curfews, rules and regulations–not unlike the military. It took a lot of energy and creativity to cause even a little leak. I was going steady and spent as much time as possible with my friends and boyfriend, Brian.

The culmination of my last year in Key West was the Junior-Senior prom night. This quickly became a very heated family debate. Everyone in my entire universe (which was not all that expansive in Key West) was going out to eat after prom at a fancy restaurant. It was a pass to stay out really late for almost everyone. Not for me. I had a strict curfew that my dad insisted was not going to change—even for prom. I begged. I cried. I pleaded. I am pretty sure I may have attempted a show of strength by slamming my door and refusing to leave my room. However, there was no compromise. All of the blossoming I had done that year must have been heading for that very moment when I, Diane Wheeler, decided that enough was enough and I was going to take matters into my own hands.

Since I was already was being forced to move at the end of the year, ripped from my friends in Key West and sentenced to live in Illinois, what did I have to lose? Even if I was going to be grounded for a year, it would be worth it to defy authority and set sail on my own. So, I decided I was staying out late after prom, no matter what the consequence. I did not even tell my closest friends what my plan was as I imagined my dad interrogating them to get to the truth.

As prom night grew closer, a group of friends and I crammed into a little dressing room of The Diana Shop, a dress shop on Duval Street. We tried on prom dresses in every color and style for as long as the clerk would tolerate us. My heart was set on a pastel yellow, flowy, georgette long gown. It was everything I ever dreamed of wearing. We oohed and aahed over each gown. We were exhilarated and filled with anticipation about this long-awaited event. My excitement may have been partly fueled by my secret plan for a night of emancipation; but the gowns were a close second place.

Alas, I would not have the long yellow gown. It did not pass the formal reviews. My mother had other ideas of what my prom dress should look like. I did not even really complain when my mom decided to take me on a shopping trip for a more sensible dress I could wear again. I was thinking to myself that I would still be grounded way into the future and there never would be another "again." And so it came to pass that my prom dress was a ballerina length white chiffon dress with splashes of big pastel flowers. It had a pink chiffon scarf that hung loose from the shoulder. Looking back at vintage styles, I realize it was a beautiful dress and much more mature and sophisticated than I would have ever picked. It was perfect for this moment in my life.

As prom approached Brian and I devised a rather bold plan, considering we didn't even have either money or our own vehicle. It was quite courageous to defy my parents and I was dauntless at promoting this event. Prom night arrived. I already had irritated my mother by rewashing and restyling of my over-teased hair after a salon visit. Fortunately my parents had a social event so I did not have to lie on my way out the door. So, as soon as they left, I amped up the eyeliner, pinned a gardenia behind my ear, and left for prom. His brother had loaned us a "Conch cruiser" complete with rust holes in the floorboards. It was kind of fun as you could see the road through the holes. It was a good thing that my father did not see my princess carriage, which was missing some essential parts, or my plan would have been foiled.

Prom in those days took place in the school cafeteria. This was the very same place where the loud and unruly students ate their lunches and gathered in the mornings before school began. I had helped decorate the space for prom, excited to have a hand in the transformation for this long-awaited event. Clouds of white and pastel balloons were billowing from the ceiling and silver glittery stars were suspended from the lights. In the center of room was a mirrored ball that scattered flecks of light all over the cafeteria. By the time my own girls were in high school, prom was held at fancy hotels, professionally decorated. Their carriages were limousines, not Conch cruisers. Still, there was something magical and also nostalgic about having our cafeteria transformed from the mundane for prom night.

Prom lived up to my expectations. Brian was wearing a white tuxedo. With a gardenia in my hair, I danced all night and mingled with friends. As the evening wore on, I slipped out of my very uncomfortable high heel shoes. I was a barefoot girl at heart and at 5'9" (175 cm) not that comfortable in heels. The music that night echoes in my memory. Rosie and the Originals played singing my favorite song, Angel Baby. Although the music was in transition that year, the Doo Wop tunes were the most memorable ones and suited the magical ambience of our cafeteria.

After prom, Brian and I did not have the money to go to a fancy restaurant so we went to the local burger place, Pizzios, and got hamburgers and fries. We went to Smather's Beach and kicked off our shoes and walked along the beach. To fulfill my goal of emancipation, my plan was to stay out late enough to make all the trouble I would soon be in worthwhile. We sat along the sea wall and dangled our feet over the side and talked for hours. In my memory, the Florida sky that night was extraordinary. It was a moonlit night and the low fluffy clouds were illuminated as they drifted over us. The stars were bright. There was a soft buzz of ebbing traffic as the wee hours of the morning approached. From time to time I had moments of apprehension and guilt, but I let them fly out of my mind. Brian and I made many promises and plans. We even talked about running away together so we would not be separated—but realized that would have been quite a stretch as we had no money and were in a borrowed car that most likely would not have made it all the way to Miami. Although we were both starry-eyed and young, we both knew we would let go and drift forward to fulfill our own individual destinies in life. Time and circumstances were not on our side. We both had larger dreams for the future. Not to mention the fact that by now I suspected my dad had probably formed a search party to capture and return me home. I knew deep inside that leaving Key West could not be wished away. Still, I also felt as if I had taken steps to become the master of my fate. I also knew that fate was about to become reality.

When I decided it was quite late enough with a sigh and feeling of resolution, we returned to the princess carriage. I let myself out down the street to keep Brian out of trouble and walked into my house alone. I was prepared for my punishment. I truly felt a little bit guilty for worrying my parents but I felt that my exercise in independence was justifiable and worth it. Not surprisingly I was reprimanded and grounded. I was now forced to spend the few weeks I had left in Key West in solitary isolation and I was rapidly spiraling into doom and gloom.

One afternoon, after school, a group of my best friends came by my house after school. They brought me a gift that I treasure to this day. It was a gold bracelet with my name engraved on it and all of their initials engraved on the back. We had a long hugging and crying session as we mourned that our time together was soon ending. I believe my mom had a hand in my compassionate end to my grounding. She knew that moving and beginning my senior year in another new school was a real sacrifice. After that, my parents never mentioned my punishment again. I ran free absorbing as much of Key West as humanly possible. I spent my days collecting images, smells, sounds and feels of Key West into my mind so I would never forget my little island.

A few weeks later, the movers arrived and I said my wrenching goodbyes. The never-ending tears became angst. I was inconsolable and angry at the world. Even though I had made great strides in my battle for independence, I knew I was not prepared to survive alone in the world and still relied upon my family. Realistically, there was no "up" side to leaving Key West and landing in Champaign, Illinois. The beautiful sea had become a flat prairie covered with corn fields, barns and silos. My friends were almost 2,000 miles (3200 km) away on my little island. I placed my conch shell on my dresser and vowed I would return home to Key West. I endured my senior year and began counting the days until I would be back in Key West. I was an outsider in Illinois and did not attend prom and had to be coerced to even attend my high school graduation. Of course, a year later we all set out to college or the "school of life," and it would never be quite the same. The world does not stand still and wait for you to return.

Wherever I walk in life, the little island I love so much is still with me. The memories do not fade and they comfort me, and the spirit of self-determination that blossomed there in high school is part of who I am today. My pilgrimages back to Key West have restored my spirit my entire lifetime. I took my first teaching job there and have returned many times to reconnect with old friends and with my little island home. I will always be that sixteen year old who escaped to walk along the beach in a prom dress that night, running free with a gardenia in her hair.

Note:

As it happened, I did see Brian again. His father was transferred to Great Lakes Navy Base in Illinois and when I was in college, we met up several times. Once again time and miles took us in different directions, fate never bringing us back together. He joined the Navy and somehow we lost touch during the Vietnam War. Fortunately, I have stayed connected with many of those friends who grew up alongside me in the Keys in the sixties and I treasure all of those who became a part of my rich life. Leaving Key West was not the end of my bond with the island or the friendships.

Swim Baby, Swim
By Diane

Magical sandbar at Bahia Honda
Photo by Nikki Pena-Infande

Between Ohio Key and Spanish Harbor Key lies a little island that captured my heart more than 60 years ago. I have made many pilgrimages back to Bahia Honda since my first visit in 1961. The old bridge, now a partial fixture, still has a spectacular view of my favorite little sand bar. Tucked away under the old bridge was my first real kiss. I had been invited to my boyfriend's family picnic and after an afternoon of swimming, we found a hiding place away from his snoopy siblings tucked under the old bridge.

Actually, being an only child, I truly loved the hustle and bustle of their family, so in retrospect, the escape was probably not my plan. The kiss was pretty short but the view was long and spectacular. I can recall many of the details of that afternoon, right down to the pineapple upside down cake and the fried chicken. I was taking home economics and had sewn a pale yellow A-line shift just for the occasion and tied my hair back with a matching satin ribbon. I may have been going for the Jackie Kennedy "look" but probably missed the mark a bit. Though it was many years ago, I still recall watching the sun slip lower in the late afternoon sky and the crystal clear water that melted into the horizon. The beauty of that balmy afternoon is etched in my memory. I have always claimed that spot as my own.

The sandbar at Bahia Honda mesmerized me in that moment and still draws me back. I return often to that spot to play in the current. I now have a large collection of memories from the many visits I have made back to that sandbar. I have enjoyed bringing my own children there to swim and behold the beauty. There is a strong current just off shore that carries you along the shore towards the bridge. I love to play in the current there, dragging a raft up the beach and drifting back down at a pretty fast clip. I have shared that sandbar with schools of fish, horseshoe crabs, sting rays and sea turtles. The sea turtles build nests on that little point of the beach. I have watched sea turtles battle their way out of their leathery eggs and struggle to make it to the water. Their determination is a sight to behold. Sea turtles go towards the natural light and hopefully are not distracted from their path to the ocean. Only about one in a thousand survives its journey. In the same way, I have drifted peacefully where the currents have taken me in my own life and also have struggled to break free from the pulls that were taking me in the wrong direction.

By the time I graduated from Illinois State University, I had been thousands of miles and seven years away from the sandbar there. I had been married and made a home in the frigid plains of North Dakota and the scorching desert of Southern California. I had given birth to my daughter and divorced. After graduating, I lingered in Illinois working for a while. All of those years, although homesick for Key West, I went with the current and accepted the flow somewhat gracefully. One day, for no particular reason, I grabbed my paddle and decided to change course. I interviewed for my first teaching position, which was on Sugarloaf Key. I happily gave away my snow shovel, the giant bag of kitty litter, and pieces of cardboard—all the necessary items to move forward in ice or snow during Illinois winters. My escape from the Midwest was fairly unpopular with my family, but I was determined to go back to the island that I was so homesick for. I heard the sea calling my name. I felt a sense of desperation to recapture a small piece of what I thought I had lost along the way. I had completed a long list of responsible things that I had been called upon to do—juggling all the pieces of my life to support and care for my child and finally completing my college degree. Now, I needed to find the free spirit again and see where this new current might carry me.

My return to Key West was almost a religious experience. I had recalled every nook and cranny of the Keys in my memory, but now I was really there. I absorbed the colors, the sounds and the salty smells that reawakened my senses. A few days after I arrived in Key West, I surprised my old friend, Billy. He lived in his family home on Fogarty and I had a little apartment on Bertha Street. He now had a treasure coin business and I was embarking on my first teaching position. That visit gave me instant "family" and I was able to easily reconnect with many old friends. I soon felt that I had never really left Key West.

Before I continue my tale, I should explain that I loved being a mom. I did, however, struggle with being perpetually tied down and left out of life's adventures. I fully understand Jimmy Buffett's "Caribbean Soul" concept. Because I was a single parent, there was no money or time to escape the endless and mandatory procession of cleaning, cooking, laundry, and work. By this time, I realized I was not fulfilled or passionate about those necessary, yet uninspiring chores. So within the first few weeks I arrived in Key West, I met a tall, blond treasure hunter, who was a free spirit traveling his own direction in life. I felt I had found a kindred spirit with the life I envied. Although it might have been impulsive, it certainly had an appeal. I took a wild leap and seized the day.

School began and I was feeling all the "growing pains" of a first year teacher. Even though the challenges were great, I instantly knew I belonged in a classroom. To somewhat complicate matters, my car that had sounded like a train for months died forever right on Flagler Avenue. I took the money from the junkyard, and replaced our mode of transportation. I invested in a bicycle and my daughter decided on roller skates. It was Key West and we were pretty inventive and undaunted by the loss of our vehicle, making it clear we belonged in the Keys.

As Labor Day approached, I was invited to an adults-only boat trip to the Tortugas with my new-found friend. I wrestled with whether I should leave my daughter for three days—something I had never done before. My inner voice might have been reluctant, but my newly-reactivated free spirit said YES! There was only one option for a babysitter and she was not the 80-year-old sensible one I had in Illinois, but, instead, a 14-year-old that resembled Roald Dahl's *Matilda*—smart and old beyond her years. Was there "uneasiness?" Yes. Did I heed that feeling? Nope. I felt entitled to one moment with the wind in my face. I said my goodbyes, with copious instructions of course, and gave my mom's phone number to the sitter for emergencies. (Remember she was over a 1000 miles (1600 km) away and already quite reluctant over my return to the Keys with her granddaughter.) As the restored antique boat left Key West and we broke out into the open ocean, I felt wildly excited about my adventure. I was busy recapturing everything I had left behind so many years before and had missed so much.

Do you believe Murphy's Law shadows you in life? Well, my father had even given me a mug with that law embellished on it. It might have been a premonition on his part. The first part of the trip was exalting. Things seemed to be going quite well and by then I had assured myself I had made a wise choice to go on this much-needed adventure. The land disappeared and I barely noticed the afternoon sky turning dark. Soon we found that we were caught in a squall out in shallow water, making the boat yaw side to side wildly. The boat pitched and rolled. We were tossed back and forth in the water and had to cling to the railings to stay upright. Fortunately, the crew was experienced and we did not roll over in the waves. Being the optimist I normally am, I refused to worry. Truthfully, I had never been on a boat in a storm and was somewhat unaware of actually how wrong things could go. Somewhere during all the lurching in the churning water, the bilge pump overheated and died. In addition, one of the engines quit working. I was a bit dinged up by then and had managed to hit my head, and sported a goose egg. (However this bump on the noggin had absolutely nothing to do with the denial I was still feeling about our situation.) The boat was taking on water rather rapidly and we began bailing.

My position was on the ladder coming from the galley where I passed the buckets up to the person on deck. In a short time, I was covered with oil and muck and had bruised my shins trying to stay on the ladder. My arms were bruised up to my elbows from hitting them on the metal when lifting the bucket. I was wishing I had done some weight training. It seemed that we bailed for hours while those with much-needed mechanical ability worked on repairing the bilge pump. We were definitely losing the battle with the rising water below. My arms ached and I only felt fortunate that I had been spared the humiliation of being seasick during an emergency. They called the Coast Guard and tried to flag down a Cuban fishing boat we saw, but we got no response.

I must admit that, by then, doubt and mild panic were beginning to slip into my mind. My treasure-hunting partner told me to go gather valuables quickly. The loudest voice in my head at that point was the one that said that my mother was definitely NOT going to understand how I had elected to leave my child with a teen babysitter and had the audacity to die in such an irresponsible manner. She would have forever blamed my move back to this latitude for my untimely death. All my years of responsible effort would be erased from memory in just one afternoon.

Thankfully, the bilge pump was repaired before total disaster. By that time, the large wooden canopy on the back of the boat had collapsed and my free spirit felt a bit shackled. We headed back towards our port in Key West in slow motion. That night, still short one engine, we anchored by the Marquesas and I slept out on the deck. My body was a bit battered and exhausted. I could not begin to remove all the sludge from my legs and hands—even with Dawn detergent. Tired as I was, I could not close my eyes, partly because of the close call with the ocean but mostly because I could not take my eyes off the millions of stars suspended over my head. Off in the distance, was a display of the lightening that had caused havoc earlier in the day.

The best moment of the evening was when the seasoned sailor and diver turned to me and said, "You are one tough girl. I was really proud of you today."

I sure needed to hear those words at that moment in my life. I knew I had rediscovered my groove. I also realized that in order to be a truly valuable crew member, I had a lot to learn about being out at sea. I was on board with learning more and signed up for a sailing course at the community college that year. I not only acquired a new skill, but also a new passion in life.

This was the beginning of the affirmation I needed. I had not lost my way or my spirit in all those years away from Key West. I felt validated that during my years of effort, I had acquired resilience and fortitude in my journey. I was excited about the beginning of what would become a 30-year teaching career. I also knew that I would survive the squalls that would surely come and I would face them standing up with my face to the wind. In fact, this had been the adventure of a lifetime. Thankfully, my mother did not receive that emergency phone call. She would have never understood that I needed to take that risk at that moment. I think I may have taken after my dad a bit. He was a risk-taker. He just did not want me to take those risks that he embraced so fully. In my usual fashion, tears rolled down my face long after the actual event ended. I hugged my daughter and felt grateful to be reunited with her again. As I tucked her into her bed that night, thankful Murphy's Law did not prevail. If I had that moment to relive, I think I would have made that same choice again with a greatly improved emergency contingency plan.

Thank you, universe, for my time on that sand bar and for letting me land in this particular place with so much beauty. Thank you for not letting life destroy my sense of adventure and trample my spirit.

Note to self

Never abandon your passion in life and when things get tough—swim baby, swim. Be that one-in-a-thousand that survives.

A Bold Move
By Diane

Watercolor by Diane

The decade after I left Key West passed by quickly. Life has a for-ward momentum and as much as we want to hold onto the past we become caught in the tides of the "now." The war in Vietnam raged on, stealing the lives and youth of many of my high school friends and kindred baby boomers. It would have been remiss not to be grateful for my own shielded life tucked away in the Midwest. This was not a gift to be wasted. I cherished my Key West memories and kept them in a safe spot in my heart. As I left home for college at Illinois State University far from my Florida friends, my sights were set on my future. I was navigating in new waters, feeling a little lost in the vast sea of possibilities. I had no idea what lay ahead in the future.

By the time I was twenty I'd been spirited off from college in the Midwest by a boyish, friendly Californian named Ron. He had blond "surfer" hair and a scattering of freckles. I began my marriage with the two suitcases I had received as high school graduation gifts. One was stuffed with clothing. The other one contained an iron, one skillet, a few towels, and a twelve piece setting of sterling silver that were gifts from my well-meaning family and friends. We had no money for fancy food but we dined with sterling silver. After Ron's stint in the military in Libya and North Dakota, we eventually returned to his hometown in Southern California. I was now almost 3,000 miles (4800 km) from my beloved Key West in my new married home and life. Brawley was a small town along the Mexican border and an oasis in the Colorado Desert.

I always thought it was a lot like moving to the set of the television show, *Happy Days*. Saturday night entertainment for Ron and I included cruising down the Main Street lined with date palms and parking in the grocery parking lot across the street from the Dairy Barn. We sat on the hoods of our cars visiting with Ron's high school friends. Many evenings I wistfully wondered where my own high school friends were. I had traded the tropical waters of Key West for miles of sand. Brawley is tucked between mountain ranges and was home to strange phenomenon such as sand storms, sizzling summer heat (110°F 43°C or more), black widow spiders and scorpions. Instead of sailing on ocean breezes, we drove sand buggies in the sand dunes at Glamis. The evening air was not filled with salt air but the pungent smells of the cattle in the feedlots. The residents there called it "the smell of money", but I would have traded it for the salty sea air any day. Despite all of this, I grew to love this little town. Neighbors became family and welcomed me into their lives.

My oldest daughter, Heather, was born there. Although I frequently longed to see Key West again, I thought of this little desert town as home. I never thought I could feel that way again about another place. Seven years later when my marriage ended, I set sail again for a new life back in Illinois near my family. When I left the Imperial Valley on a Greyhound bus, about a dozen neighbors and friends gathered at the drab little station to send us off tearfully for our new life. I was headed back to the same place this chapter of my life had begun, near my parents with a toddler to continue my studies at Illinois State University, which after all seemed to be destined to become my alma mater. Although I once again had lost a home and sense of belonging, I was inspired and excited to go back to college and become a teacher. While I lived in California, I had volunteered at a community center teaching art and I had recommitted to the plan of becoming an elementary school teacher. This path felt like the right one.

The winters in Illinois during the 1970s were renowned for blizzards where snow was measured in feet, not inches. I had scraped windows and dug my car out of snowdrifts for two years while completing my degree in education. I stuck around far longer than expected working here and there, even though there were no teaching jobs in the Midwest in that era. Since my family lived nearby in Illinois, I also decided to stay close as I was divorced and a single parent. For many years I had fought the urge to jump into my car, heading south, until I was on A1A heading towards the home I left so many years before.

One frigid morning as I was wielding the snow shovel, attempting to extricate my car from a drift, I decided in that split second—absolutely, resolutely, and without ANY doubt—that I was going to get out of Illinois and go home to Key West. I felt immediate relief at my decision, despite the fact I had no actual plan in place to make this dream a reality. My friends laughed it off and my family refused to speak of this risky endeavor. However, my mind was set.

With the help of a modest Christmas fund and a small credit union loan, a few months later I was on a plane flying to Key West. I had scheduled an interview with the Monroe County Board of Education for my very first teaching job. Luckily, I knew a few people in the system from my distant past. Since my budget was nearly depleted by travel and a place to stay, I did not even have the money for a car rental. My quest was to interview with three principals and acquire three blessings (recommendations) to be placed into a pool of new teachers for the upcoming school year.

That morning, I put on my best sundress, bemoaning the fact that I must have been the whitest, pastiest-looking person in the entire Florida Keys. Then I set off for my interviews on foot with a roll of quarters for the city bus to collect those must-have recommendations. I began at Poinciana School and worked my way to Harris School. I left my sneakers by the door of each school and put on my strappy "interview shoes" as I entered the doors with my resumes and hope. After two successful interviews, I set out for my last interview at Glynn Archer. I had to run to be there on time. When I arrived, I was frazzled and melting from the humidity that was foreign to my body after serving my time in a colder climate. I entered the school, still wearing my sneakers and my hair had turned to frizz.

Thankfully my interview was with Dr. Arnold, which sounded intimidating, but turned out to be Ralph Arnold, a very understanding classmate from high school. I was completely wilted and he offered me water, seeing my overheated distress. Despite my deteriorating state I was fortunate he also saw that I was committed to becoming a teacher and I secured my third okay for the day. Three interviews in one day on foot was actually pretty impressive, as I look back. The next day I signed my contract, exhilarated by the prospect of becoming a teacher and moving home to Key West.

The next hurdle was finding a place to live in Key West. Anyone who has ever moved into Key West must know what an obstacle that is. I had a shoestring budget and no idea where to begin. I secured a list of possible housing from the school district and fortunately the first person I called was a single mom named Beverly who took me under her wing and hauled me around in her old station wagon. My criteria was pretty basic and went downhill from basic quickly as reality set in. Rule number 1: This is Florida, land of mammoth roaches and exotic bugs. Check in all the dark places including under sinks, in closets and kitchen drawers inspecting for evidence of bugs. Rule number 2: Accept the fact that you will be paying twice as much for half the space. Lower expectations of personal space significantly. Rule number 3: Even if your bedroom is a closet, do not complain. You will be living in paradise.

I settled on an upstairs apartment right next door to my new-found friend Beverly and her three girls. It was way too expensive but it was on

Bertha Street. If you leaned over the balcony far enough, you could see the ocean. A breeze blew though the jalousie windows, making life quite bearable even without air conditioning. It had absolutely no roaches, except for an occasional renegade Palmetto bug. Recovering from the sticker shock, I immediately gave up the idea of cable television. (FYI—To watch TV in the Keys, you must have cable.) Little did I know that the water in 1980 would cost even more than the cable would have cost—although water is not so optional. Paradise comes at a high price but this rather bold endeavor had to work. After all, I had a contract to teach.

During the time surrounding the summer of 1980, 125,000 refugees fled to the Keys during the Mariel boatlift. At the same time, that July, I packed up my Gran Torino, which was literally on its last legs, and headed to Key West with my daughter, Heather, by my side. It was not a popular move with my family but I was still inspired about going home and beginning my teaching career. One curveball was that Heather had broken her arm that summer as I was preparing to move. So, she sat beside me sweltering in the summer heat with a cast on. Between us was her little gerbil, Cutie Pie. It was a long haul in the heat and humidity to the Keys with no air conditioning. Yet I was undaunted by these obstacles as I was heading back to the place I had vowed to return to. My car ended up a casualty. It only lived a few more weeks after my arrival and sadly Cutie Pie did not last much longer either and is buried in Key West. Both the car and the much-loved pet were probably collateral damage from our long, hot road trip.

Upon our arrival, life began to be transformed immediately. Heather told me we may as well have not bothered to move the silent television but she plugged it in anyway hoping for the best. In a very short time, so many other activities filled our lives, television no longer mattered much. When my car died at an intersection on Flagler Avenue, the junk yard offered me $75.00 for it. I purchased a used bike with an oversized basket. Heather opted for roller skates. We were a sight to behold traveling around Key West but we grew to love our new life and caught the spirit of the Keys in no time. Her favorite spot was the roller skating rink and mine was the beach. We went to many sunsets with friends, snorkeled, and we were taken in as family by my dear friend, Billy.

Life in the Keys was beautiful but not for the faint of heart. In 1980, there was only one desalination plant up and running when I first arrived. The water could be reduced to a trickle mid-shower, leaving you covered with soap. I hauled a paint bucket of ocean water for emergency rinses and flushes. Later that year, they opened another plant. The increased water pressure began breaking loose ancient rust, and orange water gushed from the faucets. All of our clothes were covered with rust stains but the water pressure was heavenly. And, when you have a great summer tan, rust is not a bad color to wear.

There were brief moments I wistfully recalled the days I owned a car and had a washing machine in an apartment. Laundry via bicycle/roller skates was a long hard job. I had to haul bags of dirty clothes to the laundromat in my basket. I normally had to make several trips so I would leave Heather standing guard as I returned for more dirty clothes. We had plenty of sandy, wet towels every week. I would fuel up on a *café con leche* for the return trips home. No matter how many quarters you used to dry clothes, they were never ever going to actually be dry. To save money on dryers that still resulted in damp clothes, I often opted to hang out clothes on the clothes line at our apartment. This chore entailed hauling multiple loads of heavy, wet clothes on my bike in order to hang them on my clothesline. Looking back, it was an early version of the Peloton workout. Grocery trips to Winn-Dixie were also quite a challenge on my bike. Fortunately, I had a freezer filled with fish donated by friends. My neighbor and I shared buckets of shrimp and, ignoring child labor laws, underpaid our girls to devein them. Just pedaling to the bank on payday to deposit my paycheck after work was an added stress in paradise. It was on the other side of the island and required swift action once a month!

My new friend and neighbor, Beverly, was also my mentor on how to survive in paradise. She set a high bar as she not only persevered, but did so with style. This willowy blonde, also a single mom, juggled life with a day job and also worked regularly at two side jobs. She knew how to live on a shoestring and make it look stylish. Her apartment was island "chic" and her wardrobe was filled with flea market finds that could have been on the cover of Vogue magazine. I never quite acquired her level of finesse but I wanted to believe if she could tackle life in the Keys, I could do it too. Her greatest fashion "hack" was wearing a vintage cotton slip from the local flea market as an evening dress and pinning a flower in her hair. She looked elegant and was the vision of a true island gal. I am not sure I would have made it through my first year of teaching without her expert guidance and sense of humor.

About two months into my new-found Key West style poverty, I took on a roommate, sacrificing even more of my personal space. His name was Michael and he came into our home complete with a very elderly dog he had rescued from the motel where he worked. After removing years of sand fleas, the dog relaxed in our living room. He rarely actually walked anywhere and had to be carried down the stairs. He did sport a vicious bark so we named him Killer and hoped his name would scare off any potential burglars. He was not exactly the dog of my dreams—or the roommate of my dreams either. Like every other adjustment that came along with living in paradise, it had its ups and downs.

My first official teacher meeting was held at Key West High School right in the same auditorium where I sat as a student. I was surprised to see many of the same teachers I had known 16 years before. I had one of those teary moments in life sitting there with my former teachers as a brand-new teacher. I had never even anticipated becoming a teacher, much less a teacher in the Keys. I was able to approach several and reintroduce myself and thank them for my high school years. It was an inspirational way to begin my teaching career. Many memories of high school flooded back as I peeked down those same corridors that echoed with cherished fragments of time. This moment was exhilarating for me; I was a teacher in the Keys!

When my teaching assignment was finalized, I was assigned to a position on Sugarloaf Key, about twenty miles from Key West. This was not the most convenient assignment for a person with no car. However, in the true spirit of Key West, I joined a carpool despite having no vehicle to share. This meant that each morning I had to bike to the home of whoever was driving that week. Despite my generally happy Key West state of mind, I did grumble many mornings as I had to lug my books and papers in the basket rain or shine. The worst days were the ones where I had to ride into the wind. Sometimes it was faster to walk than ride my bike there. I was wilted a bit by the time my actual workday began. I had to ignore my frizzy hair and often pinned a tropical flower in my hair to make my wild curls look intentional. Living in paradise has a price.

My carpool companions were quite pleasant and supportive. It was kind of a diverse, quirky crew of people. I won't lie, some of the people actually smoked pot on the way home from school. I was not nearly as cool as I envisioned. Truthfully, I sat by a window while praying not to be arrested during my first year teaching. This was the era in the Keys with marijuana bales and occasional bodies floating up on shore. I always say I lived in the Keys during the *Miami Vice* era. There were lots of huge drug busts and lots of people suddenly just disappeared from town and from my classroom, as well.

My class was pretty challenging that year. My student teaching and teacher preparation was conducted in a second grade class, but I was assigned to a pretty mature fifth grade class and the teachers got to select who they donated graciously to me—the new teacher. There is a vast difference between a teaching assignment in a primary grade and an upper elementary school grade. The older students come with an extra dose of attitude. Need I say more? Despite the challenges, I loved each and every student in my class and I can recall every face and name in that group even after 30 years of teaching. We all seemed to survive my first year of teaching!

The first standout moment took place when an angry student shattered the classroom window. At that moment, I felt certain that this could be the end of my two-day career but the principal had the window repaired and never even mentioned the mishap. I was hopeful I would survive my first year in the classroom with no more unfortunate events.

That year we took two memorable field trips. One involved a jovial guy named Nick who multi-tasked as a bus driver and also as a substitute teacher. I was quite fortunate that he was the bus driver for the first trip taken to the historic lighthouse and museum. I had never been in that lighthouse and now I know why. As I climbed the spiral staircase, I was paralyzed by my fear of heights midway, although I made a valiant effort to maintain some composure in front of my students. I reached a height where I could not go up one more step. Fortunately, Nick was there to rescue me for a modest price of twenty bucks that I offered him in desperation. He accompanied my students to the top of the lighthouse while I crept back down the staircase a snail's pace. I would not have lived down disappointing my students by leaving without a view of Key West I have never and will never see. Nick, the superhero for the day, would have gladly let the money slide but it was well worth that twenty dollars not to fully humiliate myself in front of my students.

Next, our grade level took another field trip, which initially I had expected to be a glorious adventure on a tall ship. It was not glorious. In fact, I would deem this as an epic field trip—but not the good kind of epic. It was a windy day and not smooth sailing. We were trapped in the hold of the ship, a very tight space, with seasick students. I will spare you a description of this memorable voyage. Since we remained below the deck for the entire trip comforting seasick students, it was not the tall ship experience any of us had envisioned. I missed all the glory of watching the wind fill the sails as we relived history firsthand. Sadly, I would only experience the beauty and grace of the tall ships from shore as I sat on the beach wistfully watching them for the next few months as they brought history alive in the Keys.

Even though my first year of teaching presented many obstacles, my students excelled that year and showed remarkable growth on their end-of-year tests. It was on one of those daily commutes the twenty miles up and down the Keys, we heard the sad news on the radio that John Lennon had been killed. My colleagues and I were all baby boomers and John Lennon was an icon for our generation. We shared that moment of sadness and shock in tearful silence. This team of teachers also gave an abundance of advice and moral support as I shared the scenic ride and soaked up the images of the lower Keys. I learned to laugh a bit over bad days with a little help from these friends who were far more experienced than myself. I never tired of watching the sky and water or the planes taking off from Boca Chica. I often thought of my dad taking off from the same runways years earlier. It was a remarkable year.

I found an extraordinary after-school babysitter for Heather near Glynn Archer School. She was a lovely, warm-hearted older woman. The living room in her home had elaborate religious shrines and she cooked wonderful Cuban foods, guava pastries, and exquisite cakes. She was the wife of a colorful Key West figure who had mysteriously disappeared. Heather, now eight years old, loved being in her home. It even occurred to me that Heather may have preferred to remain in her home, rather than coming home with me at the end of the day. This safe and fortuitous arrangement worked well until November 1980, when we had a record rainfall of 24 inches (61 cm) that unfortunately washed into her living room from the streets. In this sudden storm which brought waterspouts and torrential rains, cars were left floating in the streets of Key West. (That was one time not having a car was actually a plus.)

While my babysitter was fixing her home, I decided the money I was saving by letting Heather walk home with the neighbor girls to our empty apartment made more financial sense. My little *Pippi Longstocking* child became an "emancipated" latchkey child left to fend for herself until I arrived home. Heather was a very bright and stubborn child who loved to reinvent the rules so I worried considerably about the freedom she was being given but yet hoped for the best. This was probably not the safest option for a third grader but we were fortunate that no accidents happened that year. She surprised me with both her independence and her rather surprising sense of responsibility.

Despite all the challenges I encountered, most of my life back home in the Keys was filled with joyful and exciting moments. I fell head over heels for a handsome treasure hunter from California. Through my friend, Billy, I met Mel Fisher and other local color. I also was reconnected with many other old friends. Sometimes we all lounged around the pool at the Key Wester rubbing shoulders with unexpected celebrities. I learned how to sail, although there was no hope of buying a boat. I learned that friends with boats were both budget-friendly and presented less responsibility. I attended the second annual Fantasy Fest in 1980. Fantasy Fest is very adult Halloween celebration with all of the flair of the New Orleans Mardi Gras event. The streets and bars are packed shoulder to shoulder with partiers. Many attending are adorned with only body paint so I was actually dressed conservatively as a belly dancer. (Thank goodness for my bicycle workouts.) At this event, I had my first and last lifetime experience with tear gas as I tried to push through a crowd near Duval Street. I had a harrowing adventure, almost going down with a boat at sea. I would have not missed any of these moments in my life except maybe the tear gas. I thrived and Heather survived. When she talked to my mom, I had to monitor her calls as I never knew what little tidbits of our life she was going to share that would send my mom into a tizzy. I just pinned a gardenia behind my ear and held my head up high believing that I belonged there at that moment in time.

It had been a bold move to return to Key West. As my first of many years of teaching came to an end, I felt a sense of accomplishment and empowerment. Despite the financial obstacles, I had set a 30-year teaching career in motion. My students soared academically. All of the adjustments in lifestyle required to survive were met with resilience and even a bit of flair. I had reconnected with many old friends, soaked up spectacular sunsets, balmy nights and ocean breezes, and made many new memories on my little island home. I was torn between staying in the Keys, which seemed financially unsustainable, and leaving for a more stable life. This time I chose to leave Key West for a teaching position in Texas, which was part of the economic boom in the Sun Belt. This time I left on my own terms seeking a new beginning. My youngest daughter, Nikki, was born two years later in Texas. It seemed destiny was on my side. I cannot imagine my life without either of my daughters.

Fourteen years later, we moved back to Florida, within closer range of Key West. This move enabled us to make many pilgrimages back to the Keys. I felt as if I had landed back in paradise. We searched the internet for campsites on the water. We slept gazing at the stars and sometimes fended off the hungry raccoons that stalk the campsites. Our camping trips to Bahia Honda were legendary. We snorkeled in the crystal clear water on my favorite sand bar, ate conch fritters and Key Lime pie. We splurged on Kino sandals and frangipani perfume. My two girls and I have made many trips back "home" to Key West mingling old memories with the new ones. They patiently listened to my stories about growing up in Key West and we have added volumes of our own family stories to tell.

Reflections:

Time has been my teacher. It is perhaps unfortunate I have had to acquire wrinkles and white hair to be a bit wiser. I have become more accepting of myself and have tried to love who I am and where I am placed on this earth. I am still a dandelion, just as I was at the beginning of my life. I can put down roots and make a home wherever I am planted. Because I moved to Key West at such an impressionable age, it will always be my home. Changes are inevitable and I have had to move forward in new directions. Both professional opportunities and matters of the heart have guided my path. No matter where I live, the years I spent in Key West will continue to strongly influence my life. Where I am going is uncharted but I know where I have been and celebrate my experiences. I treasure my old friends that have remained an important part of my life and handled my missteps with gentle hands and kind words. My years as a mermaid have taught me not to battle the currents that change the course, but to drift as gracefully as possible into old age. When life gets too difficult, I just pin a gardenia in my hair and draw strength from my roots living on my little island paradise

Lost & Found
By Diane

On the steamy August day that I began my years at Key West High School, I had some very serious doubts about beginning over and finding new friends once again. The Keys had already won my heart but it remained to be seen how school in this strange new tropical paradise would go. The school itself was very different from any school I had ever attended. It had breezeways and the classrooms had open areas at the top and bottom that allowed the sultry air to circulate better. The humidity and heat gave me hair like Medusa that curled and coiled in all the wrong places. I did not begin with high expectations about making friends in this new home, but I would be surprised to discover that I would make a circle of friends that I treasure to this day. A lot of living is squeezed in those intense growing up high school years. The time flies quickly but the memories never fade.

One of those new friends was a tall, friendly kid named Billy (Tiny). I was so shy, I scarcely spoke, always using a soft and cautious voice. My own children and former students would find that more difficult to believe than the actual fact that I was actually young at one time. Billy was a local kid and did not mind hanging out with "military brats" one bit. By the time I was a junior, Key West felt like the home I never really had before. As that year closed, my father's twenty years of military service was also ending. I was faced with the most difficult move of my entire life. My father had decided to retire and we were moving back to Illinois, the home state my parents hailed from. To me it was nothing more than a place to go visit my grandparents and the family I barely knew.

I still recall being seated in the auditorium with my classmates as they ordered their senior rings, realizing I would not be sharing my senior year with my friends. Once again I would be in a new school starting over. Leaving Key West was a bitter event in my life. It left an empty place for many years to come. For the first time in all of my many relocations, I did not bounce back. To my parents' dismay, I spent the entire year writing letters and looking at old yearbooks with teary eyes. I kept in touch with many friends and lived my senior year vicariously through their letters and occasional phone calls. There is no way to sugarcoat the misery I felt that entire year.

The years plodded forward and occasionally I visited Florida, always so happy to cross the state line and always sad to leave again. I still felt misplaced in the world. I went to college in Illinois for several years and then married. We don't always have the ability to choreograph every event in our lives but life has a way of carrying you on down the road. My ties with Key West began to fade as my friends drifted into their adult lives. I had rejoined "the living" although still considered Key West my home. If I ever found a captive audience, I would speak of my time in the Keys, and my new California friends knew how I longed to go back to visit. I think I began painting then as a sort of art therapy to recall the scenes I didn't want to fade from my mind. By then, I had lost touch with almost all of my old friends.

My first daughter was born in El Centro, California. One stifling hot June day, just a few weeks after my daughter arrived, we drove up to a quaint little town in the mountains called Julian. The air was always fresher and cooler in the mountains and I was enjoying my first outing as a family. We ducked into a quaint café for a slice of apple pie and a coffee. The café was filled with people standing and waiting for a table. I glanced up, and standing by the door was a familiar face. We saw each other at the same time. It was Billy, my old friend from Key West! And he was with one of my best girlfriends from high school. The coincidence of this meeting which took place eight years later and almost 3,000 miles (4800 km) from Florida, reconnected me with the Florida Keys and many of my old friends. Had it not been for that meeting, Key West might have been lost to me forever.

Billy and I visited about high school days and caught up on the news of our lives. Billy was a gregarious fellow and had lots of stories to tell, filling me in on so much that I had missed. We shared laughter and tears as well. Many of our old friends served in Vietnam and did not return.

We continued to talk on the phone and write letters. Over the next years we never again lost touch. I survived a divorce, finally graduated from college and eventually in 1980, I moved back to Key West. Billy was my friend and became family to my daughter and me. He was my link to old friends in the Keys and we shared many wonderful times together. Eventually, I would remarry, acquire another daughter, and even though I was living far away again, Billy was always in my life. It would be many years before I was able to return home to the Keys.

When my youngest daughter was about three years old, Billy threw out a lifeline and sent for us to come and visit. She too, like my oldest daughter, learned to love Key West. Those were not easy years for me and many times I felt lost, but that visit cleared the path to once again change course in life. I regained hope and created a plan to move to West Palm Beach, Florida to teach school. My youngest daughter was in high school. We all traveled to the Keys as often as possible, camping at Bahia Honda and playing on the same sand bar I had claimed so many years before as my own.

One evening Billy passed through and visited us for dinner. We were busy ordering a high school ring for my daughter when he arrived. Her senior year was so filled with anticipation for dance team events, senior pictures, and graduation. As we sat around the dinner table that evening, I talked about how devastated I was that I did not get to remain in Key West and receive a class ring. Instead, I graduated from a high school in Illinois with almost 700 total strangers, wearing a ring from a school I had no emotional ties with.

Billy's next visit was to my house for my daughter's graduation. As we prepared to leave for the ceremony, he handed me a little parcel wrapped in tissue paper. I unfolded the paper and inside was a Key West High School class ring for 1965. The ring that I had wanted so much when I was seventeen years old was now on my finger. It is a constant reminder how valuable friendship is. A gift like that could only be given by someone who truly knows you well enough to see what lies deep in your heart. Eventually, he would travel to give me away at my wedding in 2013 to my husband.

Life is a long journey for us all and sometimes we are impatient, especially when our lives do not go as planned. Sometimes things are taken away from us, and in that moment of loss we experience pain that seems unbearable. It is only through the gift of time that we begin to see that those losses are often mysteriously rewoven back into our lives. Perhaps we earn these gifts through our tears and also through our resilience. Our life lessons give us the wisdom to see the real value of the treasure we receive. The ring I now wear reminds me how precious one true friend in life is in life's journey. The universe takes away and, if you wait long enough, it returns what you need in life to create a complete circle, embodied in my much-cherished class ring.

Now that I'm older, I have all of my memories and friendships from Key West. You just cannot take the frizzy hair or the Florida out of me no matter where I go. My life has been shaped by the wind in my face and the sand in my shoes. Once you have swum in the magical waters of the Gulf Stream and smelled the salt air, you have acquired a sense of joy that cannot be broken by events and changes life brings. I carry Key West inside me no matter where I am planted. You then have the wisdom to see life as a "lovely cruise" and can enjoy the journey. Not every prayer in life is meant to be answered in the way we hope. I am filled with gratitude that this one was answered. Sometimes what we have lost is returned in unexpected ways as a gift from the universe.

Mike's Memoirs & Adventures

Moving On
By Mike

Sometimes change proceeds slowly, almost unnoticeably. Yet in other times, it moves overwhelmingly fast as our lives change in an instant. At times, it is anticipated and predictable as we observe ourselves growing older in mirrors and across photographs. Still, special events from our past are preserved as recollections of relationships and serve as references of who we were, where we have been and how our world has changed. Our library of memories holdfast to those special times as static, unchanged reflections into our past, allowing us to revisit and relive how it once was before we and the world changed!

Diane and I are about to introduce you to the Key West we knew while growing up as teenagers in the latter half of the 1950s and first half of the 1960s. It was after Earnest Hemingway received the Pulitzer Prize for "Old Man and The Sea" (1953), but before Jimmy Buffet lost his jigger-of-salt somewhere on Duval Street (1977). It was during Fidel Castro's 26 de Julio Revolution (1959), the Cuban Missile Crisis (1962), President Kennedy's Assassination (1963) and the beginning of the Viet Nam War (1964), but definitely before Key West was a major tourist destination. Diane and I did not live in Key West at the same time, but we are bonded through shared experiences as *'Navy Brats'* (the transplanted children of reassigned Navy parents) and our indelible memories of growing up in Key West. It was our brat lifestyle that served as a catalyst, providing a unique perspective and appreciation of Key West culture, as compared with other communities where we had lived and abruptly forced to depart. It didn't take long to realize that we had been transplanted into a unique community with very proud inhabitants known as Conchs.

Surprisingly, we were readily accepted into this quiet and protective Conch community brimming with character and friendliness. We each fell in and out of teenage love several times, tested the limits of our youthful energy and became hopelessly addicted to the alluring adventures that was part of Conch life. Even Castro, the Missile Crisis and the Kennedy Assassination failed to alter those unforgettable memories of living on "Cayo Hueso" (Bone Key) or in the town of Key West. Diane and I will attempt to recreate the Key West we knew through our stories, so you too can experience how it was when the ocean was crystal clear, shrimpers and sailors inhabited Duval Street and something spectacular happened almost daily. Even though we are not *'Conchs'*, a title strictly reserved for those born in Key West, we cheerfully assimilated into a community that originated in the Bahamas as decedents of an English shipwrecked society who eventually sailed to the Keys in the 1800s. Instead, we were baptized as *'Freshwater Conchs'*; an accolade we wear with lifelong pride!

I was born in Altoona, Pennsylvania into a very large family of eleven aunts and uncles. My mother, the eldest sibling and daughter of Anna and John Lambert, helped raise most of my immediate relatives; Marguerite was an experienced mom even before I was born in 1942. My father, George, a Navy doctor, was assigned to the Marines and was saving lives on island battlefields somewhere in the Pacific during WWII. Until victory over Japan was declared, I was being raised by my mom, several aunts and uncles and my wonderful grandparents in Altoona.

After my father returned from the war in 1945, I was uprooted from the nurturing sanctuary of my grandparent's home into what was to become a gypsy-like life. Our small family was first transferred to Washington D.C., Huntington, West Virginia and then to Philadelphia, Pennsylvania. While dad was in Philly, my mom gave birth to my brother George back in Altoona and soon after we were all off to Hawaii. Anne and Mary showed up before I entered first grade in Portsmouth, Virginia. Across our youthful years, we were enrolled in school after school across the United States following dad's Navy career. This gypsy lifestyle has consequences in that one never sets down meaningful roots, and therefore, anticipates only short term relationships. I always tried to suppress the persistent reality that my friends and neighbors were unfortunately only transitory, at the whim of the Navy Department. Conversely, looking on the positive side, adversaries were also short term threats that eventually faded into fleeting characters in a past life. I often wished that I was back in Altoona surrounded by cousins and family. No such luck!

In the summer of my fourteenth year (1957), my father announced that he had been promoted to the rank of Captain and that we were moving to the US Naval Hospital in Key West, Florida. My first thoughts were to run away from home, but as reality set in, the inevitable was accepted with despair and hopelessness. As a teenager with life just beginning to unfold, it was devastating to leave Quantico, Virginia and head south to some unknown future to start all over once again. I actually cried as we passed by U.S. Marine Gate guards; glancing back to preserve yet another farewell memory.

Our first stop was at a Naval Hospital in North Carolina to visit another Navy doctor and his family who were our neighbors in Quantico. They had an attractive daughter Betty, who I had often thought about during school bus rides as hormones begin to saturate everything. After completing mandatory brief introductions to adults, Betty and I escaped to shoot a game of 8-ball at the local enlisted barracks. As her slender body stretched across the green felt to make a seductive corner shot, yesterday's trauma of leaving Quantico was suddenly pushed onto the back burner. In that moment, being with Betty was better than playing baseball or jumping on a trampoline!

The next morning after breakfast, Betty and I whispered silent good byes with our eyes as our family assembled into our 1955 Pontiac. My dad called it "The Chief". Quantico was already a fading memory as we sped off to Key West, a small island community somewhere off the southern coast of Florida. I was now looking forward, with cautious optimism, to a new life, in a new place, with new friends.

Dad did all the driving. Mom had declared years before that she would never drive as long as she lived as a fitting protest to my dad's attempt to teach her how to shift gears on a narrow mountain road in rural Pennsylvania. As a Naval Officer, my dad assumed that he was in charge and presumed to know how to mold us all into his version of future productive citizens, which included the classical music we were forced to endure as we surged forward through South Carolina, Georgia and into Northern Florida. Elvis, Little Richard and Chuck Berry songs were not even considered music. Radio static intermittently became too much for dad's classical ear resulting in a welcomed relief for all.

"CLICK", the sound of silence!

Air conditioning was not widely available in 1957 and our Pontiac was only equipped with window conditioning. In between cat naps, rest stops and long time-consuming stares out from my open back seat window, my mind wandered from friends left behind in Virginia to reading one-liner Burma Shave advertising signs posted at 100 meter intervals, and of course, Betty.

BROTHER SPEEDER
LET'S REHEARSE
ALL TOGETHER
GOOD MORNING, NURSE.
Burma Shave, N. Carolina

CAR IN DITCH
DRIVER IN TREE
THE MOON WAS FULL
AND SO WAS HE.
Burma Shave, S. Carolina

SPEED WAS HIGH
WEATHER WAS NOT
TIRES WERE THIN
X MARKS THE SPOT.
Burma Shave, Georgia

ROUND THE CURVE
LICKETY-SPLIT
BEAUTIFUL CAR
WASN'T IT?
Burma Shave, Florida

It was a long, hot, two day trip to Tampa and finally arriving in central Florida, with our destination in sight, was a welcomed relief.

The next day we finally entered the Everglades. My attention was now laser focused on catching a passing glimpse of alligators, snakes and turtles hidden in swamp grass as we sped by under an endless blue sky dotted with puffy-white clouds. We were traveling south on highway 41, also called the "Tamiami Trail" or "Alligator Alley", as it connected Tampa with Miami before Interstate 75 was envisioned. The road was only two lanes with very few service stops and we all hoped that Miami was just beyond the distant heat mirage that seemed to be traveling ahead of us at the same speed. In the late afternoon we finally arrived at a motel somewhere southwest of Miami with an inviting ocean-blue pool. Following a refreshing swim and a family dinner, it was off to bed. Big day tomorrow; Key West was just a little farther down the road, or so I thought.

Families with children always travel at a snail's pace since kids are high maintenance. There are meal stops, bathroom stops, throw up stops, stops for gas and stops for mental recovery. In 1957 there were no Rest Areas with facilities as we enjoy today. It was always a challenge to keep everyone in good spirits and dad never seemed to want to stop unless mom sounded off in our defense;

"George, they have to go!"

As we traveled south towards the Florida Keys, I now understood that Key West was the last island, in a series of islands, connected by a multitude of bridges. To my astonishment, Key West was about 100 miles (161 km) off the Florida mainland in the middle of the ocean and only 90 miles (145 km) from Cuba. As we approached the first island, Key Largo, I envisioned crossing a very long bridge to separate us from the mainland, but was surprised by how narrow and short it was. It was just like crossing a small river on a country road back in Virginia. Key Largo seemed to go on forever with stubby palm trees, thick mangroves and struggling grasses on both sides of the road blocking any view of the ocean. Maybe my parents were playing some kind of a trick on me! I recall mom talking about the movie "Key Largo", to break the environmental monotony, and how Lauren Bacall and Bogart were perfect for each other while I imagined being with Annette Funicello, the heart throb of the Mickey Mouse Club. Eventually, we approached another bridge which was much higher than the first. There was barely room for one car, but two had to fit. My dad had both hands on the steering wheel in anticipation of a close call. We all collectively held our breath as a car whizzed by with a sudden blast of wind pressure. At the top of the bridge, I could now see the turquoise blue ocean opening up on both sides of the railings. Wow! We are absolutely going to live in the middle of the ocean!

For the next 40 miles (64 km) the unending expanse of the blue ocean, dotted with small uninhabited islands seemingly balanced on the edge of the horizon, made it easy to understand how past civilizations believed that our world was flat as a pancake; it was obvious! The Florida Keys were all consuming and I was hopelessly, totally consumed. It was like nothing I had ever imagined. It was simply splendiferous!

After many narrow bridges and harrowing near misses, a road sign welcomed us to the small town of Marathon. Dad stopped at an outdoor sandwich shop where we immediately overloaded the restroom, ate a quick lunch and gassed up the car at an adjacent Texaco station. The front windshield was now clean, oil level good, tire pressure checked and everyone was happy that the end was finally in sight. We were once again off to Key West. Not paying much attention to what I thought was just another bridge, my focus changed when I realized that this bridge seemed to have no end! Dad's attention grew more serious as specks of windshield bug debris quickly grew into large trucks. Separated by a thin white line in the middle of the highway and the bridge railing, it was a choice between a head on collision or a roll over into imagined shark infested water. Like back seat ostriches, we closed off the world by squeezing our eyes shut to eliminate the possibility of a visual calamity as trucks sped by one after another. After what seemed to be a lifetime, we finally exited Seven Mile Bridge onto Little Duck Key. We were all thankful to be alive!

It wasn't long before we crossed the final bridge onto Cayo Hueso where a large billboard sign welcomed us to Key West. The US Naval Hospital, an ominous three story cement structure that could withstand a Category 5 Hurricane, was located immediately on our left. We were finally at our new home and I instantly knew my new life was going to be a great adventure!

Front Porch Recollections
By Mike

In 1948, my grandfather John and I were always the first to wake and greet the morning in Altoona, Pennsylvania. His family home was carefully carved into a steep slate slope adjacent to the 12th Avenue Steps with an elevated front porch view of the city. During winter, grandpa would carefully descend the narrow kitchen steps into the basement to shovel coal into a furnace that reminded me of a large octopus with its tubular hot air conduit arms stretching out in every direction. That scary sooty image remains with me even today.

In January, when the weather was icy cold, I would head for the front porch for a forbidden treat while grandpa was preoccupied feeding that octopus with coal in the basement. Several frosted glass milk bottles, secured in a heavy wire carrier, were routinely deposited near the front porch steps earlier by our Evens Dairy milkman. Milk homogenization was not yet adopted in Altoona where cream and milk are irreversibly mixed together to form stabilized whole milk. As a result, the buoyant sweet cream would separate from the milk and float to the top of the glass bottles. When temperatures were exceptionally cold, I would often find popsicles of rich cream oozing from frozen bottle spouts. After consuming large portions of the delicious eruptions, I unfortunately rendered the families' milk similar to today's skim milk. Nonetheless, I felt that my mother's family position, the first born of 12 children, allowed me to continue enjoying my front porch indulgence. Of course, this was wishful thinking which often resulted in silent stares as my relatives gathered around the breakfast table. As milk homogenization was rapidly adopted in Altoona, my front porch popsicles became tasteless dilutions of something that was once highly addictive. Sometimes the intentions of technology have unintended consequences, especially for kids who will never experience cold morning popsicles of frozen concentrated sweet cream!

Eventually, winter faded into spring and it wasn't long before summer was upon us with Nana, Aunt Anne, Uncle Leo and my mom making plans for our Independence Day get together. Most of my aunts and uncles had long left grandpa's home, found spouses, had kids of their own, but lived locally. As a long established tradition, everyone available would show up for dinner on July 4th, even my dad who was in Philadelphia attending a six month post Medical School training sponsored by the Navy Medical Department. He would eventually become an 'OB-Gyn' doctor during the post WWII baby boom. In other words, he would be preoccupied delivering babies during most of my adolescent life.

Nana, who was a pastry chef in her late teens, began preparing the dough for her sour cherry pies several days in advance of our July 4th dinner. On July 3rd, Cousin Joey and I began picking cherries in the back yard while our Aunts began rolling out pie dough on the kitchen table covered with a blanket of flour. As I recall, there were more than ten sour cherry trees in Nana's back yard, shallowly rooted into a perilous steep slope adjacent to our uphill neighbors.

Their daughter, Mary, often gathered neighborhood kids to play the popular street game "Mother May I" in the evenings where I would often join in. Mary was my very first heart throb, but who was also very problematic when she became "The Mother" in that silly street game. Mary intentionally directed commands to other players in a manner to catch me off guard. After waiting forever for a command, I eventually would hear:

"Michael, you may now take 3 steps forward."

In order to move forward towards the finish line, one must first say "Mother May I." Blinded by Mary's good looks and her game psychology, I often bolted forward in anticipation without uttering the "Mother May I" part and was instantly sent back to the starting position. Damn!

July 4th finally arrived that year on a Sunday with an obligatory early morning trek up the 12th Avenue hill with Uncle Leo to attend Church. After hearing a heavenly choir and the word of God, I skipped back home with shouts from Uncle Leo to slow down as I looked forward to lunch, sour cherry pie and family excitement. As we arrived, I was greeted with hugs by Aunts and Uncles all hanging out on grandpa's large front porch with a hanging bench-swing for two, several rocking chairs and a couch. The porch was the social setting for catching up, chit chats, introductions, drinking, smoking, politics and greeting neighbors climbing the steep 12th Avenue steps as they stopped to catch their breath. After escaping through the front door with a couple of red lipstick kiss marks, I immediately ran into the kitchen where I joined several aunts in a flurry of activity as Nana sipped a beer in her rocking chair while directing our Sunday dinner production. Not seeing any kids in the kitchen, I continued into the back yard where I joined several cousins consuming a sour cherry pie that was stealthily removed from a window ledge where it was left to cool. After many years of guilt, I finally realized that that pie was intended for us all along!

Grandpa first met Nana after finishing a slice of apple pie at a restaurant near the train station in downtown Altoona. John demanded to meet the person who made the best apple pie he had ever eaten. So, I owe my existence to an impromptu apple pie moment in 1906.

Around 3:00 pm there was a call for all the kids to tidy up and wash their hands for dinner. As a matter of available chairs, all the kids would eat first followed by adults. Nana's dinners were served family style, as we unsteadily passed bowls of hot food around the table. Older cousins would help the young ones until a delicious silence fell across the table.

After finishing dinner with a second slice of Sour Cherry Pie, it was time for hungry adults, who had been drawn from the front porch into the living room by drifting aromas, to finally assemble and take their place around the table. The vacated living room, hidden by partially closed pocket doors, was scattered with ash trays, smoldering cigars and half consumed adult beverages. In other words, an experimental playground for the younger generation. As I recall, after several of us sampled a few whiskey drinks and decided that they were unfit for human consumption, we took over the front porch with giggles and uncontrolled laughter for no apparent reason. Eventually, Mary appeared and we all followed her to the upper street for a game of "Mother May I."

That summer was filled with trips to downtown Altoona, outings with Uncle Leo and visits to the Kirsch Farm where I helped milk cows and ride the hay bale wagon pulled by two mules. In the mornings, grandpa, Uncle Leo and I would have coffee with evaporated milk, toast and jam. Once the toast was buttered and coated with jam, we would all dip the toast into our coffee for a treat that originated during the Depression Years. I continue to enjoy that tradition to this very day. Not only does it taste good, but it brings back those early morning memories.

Uncle Leo moved back home after he was discharged from the Air Force sometime before my stay in Altoona. He often invited me to join him on trips into the mountains with anticipated ice cream treats at road stops, or sometimes just to help wash his car in a cool mountain stream. At 5 ½ years old, that time was one of the best in my life while living with my grandparents and hanging out with my Uncle Leo.

Around 4:00 in the afternoon, grandpa and I would often retire to the back porch to listen to 'Amos & Andy' on the radio followed by 'The Shadow', 'Fibber McGee & Molly' and 'Inner Sanctum'. Radio was much more intriguing than TV since it required the listener to utilize their imagination to the fullest. In the evening, grandpa and I would often sit on the front porch and converse with neighbors who stopped to rest on a nearby landing as they climbed the steep 12th Avenue Steps. Grandpa's front porch was the true focal point of the house as it overlooked city traffic with steam trains arriving and departing on the nearby Pennsylvania Railroad. To me, it was the center of the world!

One evening after dinner I headed to the front porch, but was stopped by grandpa and told that it might not be a good idea to interrupt Uncle Leo since he had a visitor. Curiosity got the best of me, so I had a quick look out a front window and discovered that he was sitting on the bench-swing with Mary's older sister! Assuming that the real visitor had already departed, I opened the door and burst onto their scene. After Leo introduced me to Jean, he asked if I would like to go down to Hi-Way Pizza near the bottom of the steps and purchase three slices with pepperoni. I readily agreed and was given 30 cents. Hi-Way Pizza, to this day, is the best deep dish pizza I have ever eaten. The pizza line was long that evening and after about a half hour I began ascending the steps while nibbling on my pizza. As I climbed the steps, I could see Uncle Leo hugging and kissing Mary Holland's older sister. Approaching the front porch they suddenly morphed back into separate people with disheveled appearances. After handing Uncle Leo the warm pizza box, I joined grandpa on the back porch and asked if Jean was Uncle Leo's girlfriend.

"Maybe," he said. "We'll just have to wait and see."

Well, I didn't have to wait very long because Uncle Leo's schedule was mostly taken up by Mary's older sister, Jean. They spent way too much time on the front porch and the kissing and hugging seemed to go on forever!

Looking back on that July, after my dad returned to Philadelphia to continue his medical training, Uncle Leo became my older brother, a bond that has never been broken. Jean, the girl next door, eventually captured Uncle Leo's heart. Although I had to time-share Uncle Leo with Jean, I relished those back porch times with my Grandpa as we were transported by unlimited imagination into a different world inhabited by creepy monsters and situation humor. On December 1st, 1956, Mary's older sister became my Aunt Jean and quickly added five more cousins to the family clan!

Later that summer, after my dad finished his training, our family was immediately transferred to the Naval Hospital in Portsmouth, Virginia where I entered first grade that September. My incredible journey through life as a "Navy Brat" or the nomadic son of a U.S. Navy physician was about to begin in earnest. Brat life was exciting at first, but as I was forced to continually move from school-to-school following my dad's Navy career, one only puts down shallow roots since there is never a sense of belonging, like there was in Altoona. As visits with Aunts, Uncles, Cousins and Grandparents became less frequent, the desire for a real family home, rather than just another temporary house, begins to warp one's image of the future. Would I survive this crazy lifestyle at the mercy of military winds, just like a dandelion seed on the wing with a prayer?

Gate to Gate
By Mike

*U*pon arrival at our new home within the manicured grounds and gardens surrounding the Key West Naval Hospital, our family was temporarily lodged in a small cottage tucked away among coconut palms, colorful hibiscus flowers and fragrant night blooming jasmine. Our permanent quarters were occupied by another doctor's family who would be transferred to their new duty station in a few weeks. From the cottage porch, I could easily throw a rock into the Stock Island Channel which was held back by a three foot cement seawall and adjacent sidewalk. My initial days were occupied watching brightly colored angel fish display their colors in refracted sunlight, sluggish horseshoe crabs crawling through swaying sea grass and blueish green needle gars that darted to and fro on the water's surface as I curiously peered over the wall. The shallow water was hypnotically inviting, crystal clear and perfect for snorkeling. However, I would first need a mask and fins before I could breach a perceived vulnerability boundary to enter into their weightless domain. Barracuda and shark encounters were realistic possibilities out in the main channel, but the presumed safety of the shallows was somewhat reassuring. Nevertheless, the lure to explore my new underwater environment was beginning to take hold.

One morning while walking along the wall, I met a cute eighth grader who lived in the house that I would eventually call home. In a shy way, Kathy and I became friends as we exchanged details and stories of our past brat lives over the days that followed. We often visited the hospital PX store that sold ice cream, candy, magazines, toiletries and an assortment of skin diving equipment priced way beyond my ex-paperboy means. Nonetheless, I made detailed mental notes of exactly what I would need to swim alongside my fishy friends, including the price: mask ($5), fins ($7), snorkel ($1) and a spear gun for predator defense ($15). Asking my parents for $28 was totally out of the question in 1957. However, with the will and a plan, there may be a way. I could just ask for $6 to get started with the essentials; a mask and snorkel. My perceived future adventures were underway!

After receiving my new Dependent Navy ID card, Kathy and I boarded a city bus and set out for downtown Key West and the Officer's Swimming Pool located on the Naval Base at the far end of our 7 square mile (18 sq. km) island. Once outside the hospital's guarded gate, the sanitized military environment quickly evaporated as we boarded an open air bus joining a scattering of passengers, some with fishing poles who were speaking Cuban at the speed of light and laughing up a storm. Since I was unfamiliar with Spanish, their strange words seemed to blend together into a verbal fog.

A mile or so up Flagler Avenue, Kathy pointed out Key West High School (KWHS) where I would enroll as a freshman in a few weeks. Looking back, high school was mostly an entertaining social experience with constant academic struggles due to misplaced priorities, such as learning guitar, skin diving and peer pressure beer drinking. Report Card time was no fun! My dad had great expectations for his first born son, but I guess it just wasn't in the cards back then when I was clueless about what lies ahead in life. I was a day dreamer with a vibrant imagination that was out of sync with the life planned by my dad, the MD. My mom, a professional artist before family life took hold, was much more relaxed about my future and always told me that I was much smarter than my embarrassing grades portrayed. Thanks mom!

In a few minutes, we turned right from Flagler Avenue onto White Street which was lined with small homes, local shops, Bollito venders (black-eyed pea fritters) and the Gulfstream Market. Eventually, I would work at that market, learn to speak a little Cuban, meet some unforgettable characters and take part in several life jarring adventures.

After crossing Truman Avenue, our bus stopped to allow the fishermen to exit as they continued to talk up a storm in Cuban. I was already looking forward to signing up for a Spanish class at KWHS so I could understand and converse with locals. Within a half mile, we turned left onto Eaton Street and entered the old section of Key West with majestic Victorian homes, lush tropical gardens and Royal Poinciana trees with clusters of red flowers artfully overhanging the roadway. Frequent whiffs of pleasing tropical fragrances provided a feast for all my senses while viewing these well-kept homes. Eaton and adjacent Caroline Streets were totally different from the East end of the island where we boarded the bus. Years later, I would always stay in this section of Key West for High School reunions to enjoy early morning walks down secluded alleys and peaceful pathways filled with memories, flowers and lazy cats on doorsteps.

Kathy prematurely ended our bus ride on the Gulf of Mexico end of Duval Street near Sloppy Joe's Bar and the shrimp docks so she could show me downtown. In a few years, I would have a beer at the bar Hemingway made famous since ID checks were rare in 1959. Key West was not a tourist destination in the 1950s and the ABC (Alcohol Beverage Control) folks from Miami didn't care much to travel the 100 miles (161 km) of narrow and dangerous roads to pull off a surprise raid. In truth, there were very few ABC raids probably due to heads-up phone calls from upper key bar owners that the feds were on their way. This end of Duval Street was a little rundown with several vacant lots, small shabby businesses and many seedy sailor and shrimper bars.

As we continued walking, Kathy pointed out the striking stained glass windows of Saint Paul's Episcopal Church, a large structure on the corner of Eaton Street that seemed to serve as a sentinel separating the blue collar section of Duval Street from downtown Key West. Situated imme-diately adjacent to the church was the Elks Club where I would often attend Friday night teen dances with friends. Sometimes I would have a beer in the parking lot during a band break in an attempt to harness enough courage to ask a girl to dance. I was not a great dancer and some-times it took some liquid reinforcement to get me going. One night while waiting for the band to return, I was watching others dance to recorded music with an accentuated Cuban Salsa beat which was way beyond my dancing capability. Suddenly, out of nowhere, this young woman in a tight-fitting red dress just grabbed me and said,

"Let's Dance!"

Before I could say anything, I was in the middle of the floor dancing as if I had grown up in Havana. I just relaxed, letting the music take over. It was a magical moment as I glided across the dance floor being held close and artfully guided by exceptional skill and beauty. Then, just as I was beginning to enjoy being captured by this lovely dream, she was ripped from my arms by the bouncer and escorted out of my life. Somehow, she gained access to the teen dance from the adjacent Elk's bar that was only separated by an unguarded opened door. Later, she peered through the doorway, smiled and waved goodbye. I often wondered who she was and with whom she was really dancing with out there in the middle of that floor.

Across the street and down a few blocks we approached the La Concha Hotel, then considered one of the best restaurants on the island. With white tablecloth dining adjacent to large open-air windows, it was the after church destination for many upscale Conch families. Mixed aro-mas from the kitchen, strong Cuban coffee and Havana cigars aligned my senses to new smells as we walked slowly by to observe relaxed clientele enjoying lunch seasoned with boisterous conversation. To this day, the scent of expresso, especially with lime, instantly transports me back to Key West.

Crossing Fleming Street, we strolled past the everyday window displays in the Kress Department Store that would eventually become Jimmy Buffett's Margaritaville in about another twenty years, long after I graduated from KWHS in 1961. Approaching the center of downtown Key West, the pedestrian traffic became much more intense as we navigated our way among small groups of Navy sailors in white dress uniforms, Cuban shoppers and kids of all ages. Kathy pointed out the Monroe Movie Theater across the street with its pastel colors of pink and blue that displayed Jailhouse Rock starring Elvis on the marquee. I wasn't much of an Elvis fan, but I would enjoy many Saturday afternoon matinees with friends in the years ahead. Hot dates were better suited for the drive-in theater on Stock Island where privacy wasn't perfect, but the back seat environment more favorable for a kiss or two.

While still observing the colorful theater, we abruptly turned west onto Southard Street which was lined with repetitious shops and businesses that catered specifically to the Navy. After crossing Whitehead Street, I immediately noticed several Marine Corps guards at the Main Gate standing smartly, sometimes saluting officers, while directing traffic in and out of the Navy Base. Near the main gate, the left side of Southard Street was lined with sidewalk shoe shine venders at the ready to create a shine. The shoe stands consisted of elevated chairs with places to rest one's feet. Popular music was always playing and the venders were usually black men who shined shoes while popping polishing rags to the beat of the music. When their chairs were vacant, the venders danced about to the music. It was just something entertaining to behold while raising smiles; it was an impromptu engaging performance! Even though segregation was well established in Key West before I arrived, Conchs and Blacks respected each other in contrast to what was happening in the Southern States.

Kathy and I flashed our Dependent IDs to a Marine guard who then motioned us onto the Navy Base. Soon after my twenty-first birthday, I would become a Marine as I always admired their discipline and esprit de corps during my brat life. Actually, there is much more to that story, but for now, let's just say it eventually happened! Key West and the USMC would change my life forever! Once a Marine, always a Marine … Once a Conch, always a Conch! OK, in my case, a Freshwater Conch since I wasn't born and raised in Key West.

The Officer's Swimming Pool was a collective meeting place for the dependent children of Naval Officers. In the military, social segregation between Officer and Enlisted ranks were encouraged for families, but stringently enforced among career personnel to maintain the integrity of absolute discipline. Having friends on the other side of this and other synthetic military boundaries, always made cross-rank friendships socially difficult. It was just part of brat life living and the swimming pool was no exception.

The pool was 25 yards (22.8m) long and maybe 15 (13.7m) wide with a diving board on the deep end and wading for children at the shallow end. The reflected bottom color was a light tint of blue lined with black lane stripes. Burgers, fries and ice cream were available at a snack bar that was centrally located between dressing rooms with welcoming wooden picnic tables on the opposite side of the pool in a shaded grassy area. After emerging from the men's dressing room in my brand new swimming suit, I looked for Kathy, but she was nowhere to be found. You know, girls always take a little longer. Over the next few years I would come here often to meet friends, look at new batches of brat girls and sometimes get involved in activities that that were unbecoming of a Boy Scout who reached the rank of Star back in Quantico.

One day Joe, Michael and myself, all Navy brats, decided to make a batch of stump juice out of coconut milk, papaya juice and several key limes. I was more or less an observer in this process since they seemed to know more about the devil's brew than I. Of course, we added some yeast to our concoction to insure that alcohol, the drug of choice, would be included. According to some unknown WWII recipe from the Pacific, the concoction had to be buried for a week, in a cool place, for fermentation to proceed. After a week, we resurrected our hellish creation with anticipation of a teen age cocktail hour. As my glass was filled with the slimy liquid created somewhere outside our solar system, the repulsive smell made my face squint in rejection. It was worse than a week old dead fish! That evening we decided that our unsuccessful efforts should not just be flushed away, but rather put to good use in the BOQ (Bachelor Officer's Quarters) air conditioning system. Boy Scout training notwithstanding, we definitely were not working on a Merit Badge.

Suddenly, Kathy was swimming towards me and I took notice that she was well on her way to becoming a high school heart throb. We had a wonderful day at the pool and I could feel the sun on my back during the bus ride home. In a week, Kathy would be gone forever to find different friends in a different place. This is just how Brat Life goes and how brats evolve into adults. We all know how to handle change, but what we want most is to have a permanent home with everlasting friends.

A Chance Encounter
By Mike

Por aqui, dinero por favor!

In early August 1957, our family finally moved into our new quarters at the Key West Naval Hospital, a stone's throw from Highway US 1 and the Stock Island Bridge. Soon thereafter, everyone on the Keys was instructed to receive a precautionary inoculation against some unknown biological threat. It probably had something to do with our water supply which was piped in from the mainland. Anyway, I was not particularly overjoyed with the prospect of having a long needle stuck into my arm, but I also knew that there was no way of avoiding this dilemma. As I took my place in a long line stretching around the outside of the Naval Hospital, I would lose composure when approaching the medical station with needle-armed nurses and return to the end of the line to recover and reassess my anxieties. The more I thought about that needle, the more I needed any excuse to delay the inevitable.

After joining the Marine Corps in 1964, surviving Parris Island Boot Camp and graduating from USMC Electronics School in San Diego, I joined the 11th Marines at Camp Pendleton, California as a Microwave Radio Relay Technician. As Viet Nam began to heat up, our regiment was transferred to Okinawa, Japan for additional training including some hellraising liberties … Amen! Several weeks before departing Okinawa for Nam, I found myself once again in a long line to receive a series of inoculations and vaccinations against everything under the sun. As I approached the Medical Staff armed with high-tech injection guns and low-tech needles, old fears were somewhat tempered by military life, and besides, I was looking forward to eating lunch with some fellow Marines. Suddenly a 2nd Lieutenant cut in line directly in front of me claiming a privilege granted to officers. This cut was completely acceptable since Marine Officers answer to a higher authority, but as he dropped his trousers and underwear exposing his front row anal orifice to all, I inadvertently uttered,

"Now, there's a real ***hole!"

Of course, my conscious mind was referring to the exposed raw biology and not the person, but my unconscious companion seemed to subliminally express a different opinion. Since he was receiving an extra-large injection of gamma globulin in his naked left cheek, he could only give me a penetrating stare from his inverted position which I knew was an ominous warning. Luckily, after recovering full dressed status, he abruptly exited without a second glance in my direction. I knew that was a close "Court Martial" call.

As I approached the Key West needle-armed nurses once again, I noticed a dark complexion kid about my age exit the line just before the nurses. I watched him meander around for a while among some coconut trees, eventually taking up a position at the line's end, like I had done several times before. Relieved that I was not the only chicken in line, I decided to join the barnyard wanderer assuming that we both shared the same fear of needles. He was about my height (5' 7" or 170 cm) and weight (95 lbs. or 43 kg) with jet black hair with a slight top curl, and probably of Cuban descent. Bobby and I slowly got to know each other as our get acquainted conversation seemed to suppress the fear we both shared. Before I knew it, we received the inoculation without incident and breathed a sigh of relief. Bobby was a Cuban "Conch" and had lived in Key West his entire life. For me, this chance encounter was the beginning of a new life with many incredible Key West adventures ahead!

While standing in line, I discovered that Bobby often went diving locally for Caribbean Spiny Lobster; better known locally in Cuban as "Langosta".

He reassured me that the lobsters in Key West had no pinchers and that they were easy to gig with a trident-like barbed fork extended on a short wooden pole. Our conversation continued at the bus stop just outside the Naval Hospital gate as we waited for his ride home. I confided that I had plans to purchase skin diving equipment, but unfortunately the cost was beyond my reach. Bobby then suggested that I join him Saturday to masquerade as Key West natives where we would dive for coins dropped from waiting tourists aboard the Havana Ferry. I asked if he thought I was tanned enough to pass as a native. He reassured me that only our heads would be above water and that the tourists traveling to Cuba have lots of money and will throw coins to watch us dive as time-passing entertainment. I readily agreed, but never thought in a million years that I would be a posing as a native kid diving for coins as seen in Hollywood movies!

Key West was not a tourist destination in the 1950s due to narrow roads, many hazardous bridges, limited lodging, scarce restaurants and unsavory bars. Duval Street was usually populated with sailors, shrimpers, local characters and hometown Conchs. The only famous watering hole that survived into the 21st Century was Sloppy Joe's Bar. Instead, most tourists drove directly from Miami to neighboring Stock Island where they, along with their vehicles, were boarded onto the Havana Ferry for a 90 mile (145 km) trip to Cuba. Key West was in no position to compete with the casinos and night life of Havana. During that time, Key West was the undiscovered paradise of my childhood. Life moved at a snail's pace with magnificent sunsets, evening baseball games, warm afternoon rain showers and the comfort afforded by a community of friends and neighbors. But if one ventured into the crystal clear waters surrounding the outer Keys, that childhood comfort would quickly dissolve into an adult maturity that required a heightened awareness of curious predators with sharp teeth.

On Saturday morning, I met Bobby at the hospital bus stop wearing a bathing suit, T-shirt and an old pair of sneakers. Bobby was similarly dressed, but instead of a store bought suit, he wore an old pair of cutoff jeans. I immediately felt a little over dressed as an impromptu native diver. As we walked across the Stock Island Bridge, I pointed out the back of our new Navy Hospital home which was protected by the continuation of that cement seawall where I first encountered brightly colored angel fish and other strange underwater inhabitants. Bobby mentioned that Langosta love to live under seawalls and that I should probably pick up a gig to provide dinner for my family. I took that suggestion seriously and it wasn't long thereafter before I made my mom happy with several fresh lobster for a family dinner.

Gigging Langosta is now banned in the Keys and many countries around the world in order to maintain a viable lobster population, marginalize creature cruelty and to encourage sportsmanship. However, in the 1950s gigging was an accepted practice since Moray eels and Langosta always seemed to hang out together under coral heads and seawalls. As the story goes, a Moray eel could strike like a snake and lock onto your arm with ice pick-like teeth as one reached for that delicious lobster dinner. Being held underwater by a slimy green serpent imbedded in the coral, one had to relax to allow the eel to release and retreat. True or not, at 14 ½ years old, I had no intention of visiting Davy Jones in his Locker with most of my life, yet to be lived. Yes, I was a gigger!

As we walked towards the docks where the Havana Ferry was moored, Bobby proceeded to teach me a little Cuban to make our monetary endeavor a little more rewarding. I was instructed to say,

"Por aquí, dinero por favor" and "Gracias", for "Over here, money please" and "Thanks".

I continually repeated the strange words with corrections until they were almost automatic. Bobby said that I was a natural for the Cuban language. Before I knew it we arrived at the dock terminal and I was astonished by the size of the ship called the City of Havana, a converted Navy LSD (Landing Ship Dock) painted white. All along, my mental image of the Havana Ferry was a much smaller vessel as seen in Hollywood movies, so nervous apprehension began to set in. Bobby reassured me that we would be fine and to follow him to a safe place to enter the water. As we slowly swam towards the ferry in the 80° F (26.7° C) degree water, I could see passengers on the deck pointing at us as we approached the hull.

"Por aquí, dinero por favor", Bobby shouted!

Suddenly, silver coins began splashing all around us as we instinctively dove to retrieve our booty. We had no goggles or fins, but the flash of reflected sunlight from the sinking coins, like leaves falling from a tree, allowed us to easily retrieve the coins. This was too good to be true and at times we had to let pennies sink to the bottom in order to maximize our reward. Soon it became evident that the City of Havana was about to depart and my first Key West adventure was coming to an end just before 11:00 am. Like in poker, you don't count your money until the passengers wave good-by! The accounting process continued as we walked home and as I recall we harvested about $5 in coins which we split. The City of Havana made its final trip to Cuba in 1959 after Castro took over the Cuban government, but by that time, my Saturday mornings were filled with more interesting adventures of the heart, diving at Sand Key and learning to play guitar.

While waiting with Bobby at the hospital bus stop with a bulging pocket of coins, he invited me to join him at a party that evening near the Naval Hospital. He said it would be fun, and besides, I would meet a lot of my future KWHS classmates. We agreed to meet at the party as Bobby provided some general directions by pointing across a vacant field. He didn't know the exact address, but that I would hear the party as I approached a small cluster of isolated homes. After Bobby boarded the bus, I spent the remainder of the afternoon setting up my Hallicrafter short wave radio so I could continue listening to amateur radio conversations and the beeping Sputnik satellite. Unfortunately, the radio was wasn't working that well without an antenna, so I put it aside for when I had more time to resolve the problem. Right now I was more concerned about what to wear to the upcoming party and gaining permission to attend from my parents.

Approaching the general area where Bobby pointed, I began to hear music and muted voices echoing within the neighborhood. I decided to wear my black jacket with a junior varsity basketball letter, a red and yellow "Q" for Quantico, Virginia; our last duty station. It wasn't an actual letter jacket like those reserved for varsity sports, but it was something that I was extremely proud of and would hopefully mark me as an athlete. Arriving in the front yard, I introduced myself as Bobby's friend and asked if he was around. While waiting, one of my future classmates approached, looked at the "Q" and said,

"What does the 'Q' stand for, Queer?"

Well, it wasn't long before John and I were in a physical confrontation, eventually rolling in a ditch with arms and legs entangled in some weird wrestling hold. Finally, separated by Bobby and others, I decided to ditch the jacket while attempting to reconstruct my composure. John and I were classmates until graduation in 1961, but never became close friends. However, we were also not enemies. As a result of the "Q" incident, we instantly acquired that social quality that sometimes takes years to develop … Respect!

I would eventually come to realize that many Key West athletes were scouted and went on to play college and professional sports after winning many State of Florida championships. These kids, from a small island community of 12,000 inhabitants, had been playing sports together since grade school, were well coached and bonded together through team accomplishments. My JV Letter announced me as an outsider by way of confrontational consequences. I immediately retired that jacket and never wore it again; even though it would be my singular athletic award.

On my first day at KWHS, several classmates I met at the party waved hello with a friendly smile as we passed each other in the halls. It was a relief not to be rejected as an outsider and I began to feel as if I actually belonged.

The Girl with No Name
By Mike

It was finally summer! Well, it's almost always summer in Key West, but it was my first Saturday after finishing my final exams at Key West High School (KWHS). I would be a sophomore in the fall and it felt good to have the entire summer ahead of me with no homework or schedule; other than skin diving with friends, chasing girls and social hot dogging on Duval Street. I could hardly wait to get started.

After a late breakfast with several siblings, mom said that my dad wanted me to help him with his car, a 1955 Pontiac he called the Chief. This request was viewed by me as highly unusual and I felt somewhat ominously uncomfortable. My father and I were not on the best of terms as my school grades were below his expectations. Actually, it was much worse than that. My entire life was far below his expectations. His primary concern was cemented in academic excellence, an accolade I would not achieve until attending college following an honorable discharge from the Marine Corps, ten years into the future.

Approaching the Chief, my dad struggled with a smile and asked if I would help him service his car at the nearby Texaco Station. I was a bit perplexed by his smile, but I knew once he received my final report card grades, that smile would become a distant memory! Anyway, I agreed with suppressed apprehension as I was never encouraged to participate with dad on Navy sponsored fishing trips attended by siblings and friends. Even if I had been invited, I would have declined due to his constant public criticism of my academic shortcomings. Maybe dad just wasn't feeling that well today and really needed my help since he suffered from chronic heart disease. Not that I had a choice, but I agreed to help.

We drove directly to the nearby Texaco Station, only a quarter mile from our home, stopping the Chief adjacent to a vacant gas pump. Dad asked if I knew how to pump gas. I shrugged my shoulders to communicate "a maybe" since I often watched others remove gas caps and pump gas. After receiving specific instructions on how to properly remove the gas cap, reset the gas pump to clear a previous customer's amounts, pump fuel without overflowing and reinstall the gas cap, I proceeded to fill dad's car with high-test gas. After securing the gas cap, I looked forward to a quick ride home so I could restart my summer activities. However, dad now asked if I knew how to check the tire pressure. After more detailed instruction on how to accurately measure air pressure with a tire gauge, inflate to the correct pressure and reinstall the protective nozzle cap, I proceeded to checked all four tires, plus the spare in the trunk. Now, I really was ready to jumpstart my first Saturday of summer freedom and presumed that we were finished servicing the Chief.

Then, suddenly dad opened the hood and asked if I knew how to check the oil and automatic transmission levels, battery water and coolant. After more detailed time-consuming instructions, with repeated warnings to slowly release the cap on the pressurized coolant, I proceeded to execute his instructions; but now with a renewed interest in gaining some practical knowledge about engines. Although, not realizing it at the time, this educational happenstance with my father would stand out as a rare salient moment of what could have been in our father-son relationship. After washing all the Chief's windows I began to realize how much work was involved in servicing a car. As I was once again getting ready for our ride home, dad introduced me to Mr. Zeller, the owner of the gas station. Mr. Zeller was about the same age as my dad with a full head of gray hair, a neatly trimmed gray mustache and a medium build. He smiled and said that he was impressed by my vehicle service abilities. I also smiled, readily accepting his complement. It was at this point that I suddenly understood what was going on all along as dad informed me that I was now working for Mr. Zeller and that he would see me at dinner. Sometimes, smiles can be deceiving!

I think Mr. Zeller was also completely surprised when he realized that my dad failed to inform me that my employment had been prearranged. Mr. Zeller invited me into his office, bought me a coke from a vending machine and helped me complete documents related to my instant employment. I would earn $0.45 per hour and work 24 hours per week servicing vehicles at the gas pumps. My primary responsibilities were first to greet the customer, pump gas, check engine oil levels and wash the front windshield. Mr. Zeller and I worked together all morning as a team as he guided me along with friendly guidance and subtle humor to build my confidence. I easily mastered washing the front windshield without leaving streaks, then moved on to manually pumping gas and eventually checking engine oil levels on the dip stick. There was a lot to learn as gas caps were sometimes hidden in crazy places and engine hood latch locations were different on most models. After another cold coke with peanuts for lunch, I was on my own, but under the watchful eye of Mr. Zeller while he attended to other duties. As my mind settled, I began to realize that my new reality wasn't as bad as originally thought. At least my abbreviated summer activities with friends would now be enjoyed with earned income.

After lunch, I tried to look busy by making sure that the windshield water trough was properly filled and the paper towels dispenser was adequately stocked. It wasn't long before my first customer pulled up to a vacant pump.

"Good Afternoon Sir, regular or high-test?" I said with measured confidence.

While filling his 1955 Chevy with $5.00 of regular gas, the customer opened the hood and began checking oil and coolant levels on his own. After finishing and closing the hood, he visited the rest room while I washed both front and back windows. Upon his return, he paid $5.00

to Mr. Zeller and thanked me for washing his windows. As I would soon discover, most male drivers preferred to check their own fluid levels as knowledge of engine maintenance was respected and spun into conversations to impress peers. However, female drivers usually wanted me to check as much as possible within the time available. They always seemed to be in a hurry to be somewhere, but a clean front windshield was always a gender priority!

Over the next few days I met Jake, a part-time mechanic who performed tune-ups and small repairs, and Julio, who oil-sprayed the undercarriage of cars and helped me with customers when things got busy at the pumps. Mr. Zeller and Jake handled all the money transactions as cash was the only payment method in 1958. Eventually, I was allowed to collect payment, but never to make change or make cash register deposits. I soon became more comfortable with my new responsibilities and my knowledge of servicing different models of vehicles increased exponentially with help from my coworkers. I slowly became part of the Zeller's Texaco Station team. Even though I would be "carless" until 1967, I could hold my own in mechanical conversations with peers which helped improve my social status.

During my second week of summer employment, a red 'Ford Fairlane 500' pulled into the station with a Florida license plate not registered in Monroe County. All Monroe County plates, including the City of Key West, started with the number "38" and this vehicle was obviously from mainland Florida. After fueling the vehicle and checking the oil, I instinctively began to wash the driver's front windshield which was smeared with streaks and fragments of splattered bugs. At first I was totally fixated on removing the biological debris when suddenly a female finger from the inside passenger's seat pointed to a bug I had missed. My eyes intriguingly followed that finger until I was focused on a very cute girl with an engaging smile. She was about my age and we began playing a silly game of finding the bugs. Moving to her side of the windshield, we continued playing the game, but now my view of her was much closer and more direct. Not realizing that she was revealing much more that she realized, as my focus instantly transferred from the biology on the windshield to the breathtaking biology in the front seat. I was like the proverbial deer in the headlights, unable to move. Snapping out of my trance, I checked the windshield for streaks and then moved over to her opened window to clean the side mirror.

"Where are you from?" I asked, silently considering heaven as a possibility!
"St. Petersburg," she responded, with a smile.
"Is this your first time in Key West?"
"Yes, we are staying at the Casa Marina and I'll be here for a week."

As her parents approached the car, I quickly ended our conversation, closed the vehicle's hood and stood idly by as she departed with a wave. My flirting heart was filled with anticipation, but I forgot to ask her name!

The Casa Marina hotel was located at the far end of the island, about two miles away. As soon as I got off work, grabbed a bite to eat and cleaned up a bit, I headed out to find the girl with "no name". The hotel was built by Henry Flagler in the 1920s and was designed to accommodate wealthy travelers arriving in Key West via Flagler's overseas railroad. The railroad spanned the Florida mainland to Key West by constructing 42 bridges, the longest connecting Knight's Key to Little Duck Key known as Seven Mile Bridge or the 8th Wonder of the World. The Casa Marina opened on New Year's Eve in 1920, several years following Flagler's death. The Overseas Railroad was destroyed in 1935 by a Category 5 Hurricane and was eventually replaced by the Overseas Highway, US 1.

As I approached the enormous hotel on a wide promenade canopied with coconut palms, a seemingly endless series of double arched glass windows were slowly revealed on either side of a massive glass entry door stationed with uniformed hotel employees. Entering like a presumed hotel guest, I began exploring a large cavernous first floor sitting room with dark wood ceiling beams supported by ebony pillars cut from huge trees. The dimly lit room featured comfortable furniture, large tropical plants and a grand piano off to one side. It soon became obvious, just like Dorothy in the "Wizard of Oz", that I was in a different realm and no longer in "Kansas". Immediately, I felt as if I didn't belong and an uncomfortable apprehension began to settle in. Not knowing what to do next, I decided to look for the Red Ford Fairlane in the parking lot. No luck, it just wasn't there. Giving up and feeling that my afternoon escapade was doomed from the start, I decided to visit my friend Bobby who lived across from the cemetery on Margaret Street before taking a bus home. After telling Bobby and his mom a modified version of events, they laughed and offered me a plate of black beans and rice. My desire to meet up with that cute girl with "no name" would no longer be considered a complete waste of time, since Bobby's mom made the best "Frijoles Negros" in Key West.

I spent many hours at Bobby's house over the years and usually there was a large pot of black beans simmering on the stove. Back in the 1950s, black beans were purchased in one pound bags for about $0.50. The beans had to be soaked in water over night or longer and then cooked with seasoning and a ham bone for many hours until softened and concentrated through evaporation. The process and preparation was well worth the wait and the kitchen smells were as delicious as the beans.

While attending my 50th KWHS Reunion, I had a chance to talk with Bobby's Mom and told her how much I loved her Black Beans and Rice and especially spending time in her kitchen. I said that I now have my own recipe using ready-to-cook canned beans rather the dried version. She readily confessed that she also has switched to canned beans and we both had a good laugh. I thanked her for revealing the secret ingredient she told me about back in High School … Olive Oil.

(See recipes for Frijoles Negros and other Cuban Dishes in the Table of Contents)

My summer at the gas station was filled with several heart pounding windshield moments and many others where I was preferentially focused just on removing smashed bug biology. In either case, I always took pride in leaving customers with spotless windshields. Eventually, I learned how to drive manual shift vehicles into the service bay and position blocks under the frame for lifting, enabling Julio to oil spray the undercarriage to inhibit rust from ocean salt deposits. Lifting a Packard was the most fun of all since it had an electronic suspension that always maintained the car on a level plain. As the Packard began to rise on the lift, electric suspension motors were continually activated to maintain a level state. It was an amazing vehicle with advanced technology. Sometimes, Julio would let me oil spray during idle times when gas pump customers were at a lull. However, breathing in used engine oil was not one of my favorite pastimes!

One memorable warm day in mid-August, Jake and I were having fun squirting each other with water hoses when Mr. Zeller suddenly showed up. After lunch he called me into his office and informed me that he was letting me go. He said that he should also fire Jake, but that he couldn't because he was a valuable asset to the viability of the station. He thanked me for my service with a smile and informed me he would tell my dad that education, being more important than work, was the reason for ending my employment. He wished me success in school and not to become too focused on the opposite sex. Evidently, Mr. Zeller was watching while I was prolonging some passenger-side windshield washings!

Thus, ended my first employment in Key West. What began with a smile also ended with a smile and as I walked home my world was in a good place.

Infamously Uninformed
By Mike

It was just another regular mid-week day at the Gulfstream Market on White Street, a small neighborhood grocery store in Key West, where I was working a summer job. On that particular morning, after unloading a supply truck, restocking shelves and filling about fifty one-pound bags of black beans, the store was getting ready to open. "Frijoles negros y arroz" or black beans and rice is the traditional Cuban meal and filling those bags for customers was a daily routine. I eventually learned to love black beans and rice, but bagging those legumes was too repetitious and mind-numbing for a 16 year old.

I was in no particular hurry to arrive at my station near Pete's cash register at the front of the store, as mornings were usually slow immediately after opening. I leisurely strolled into place, while tying a fresh white apron around my waist.

"Buenos Dias Pete, Como Estas?" I said, as a matter of fact.
"Muy bien, Mike." Pete responded.

With that greeting and response, I was ready for the first customers of the day. Many Gulfstream customers had continued family ties in Cuba and only spoke broken English. Cuba has persistently influenced the culture, food and spoken language of Key West through constant migration due to their adjacent location, war with Spain in the 1870s and escape from Castro's Cuba in the last half of the 20th Century. Therefore, I was simply trying to improve my Cuban in an effort to help customers and blend in as a local "Conch", a highly regarded accolade for a person born and raised in Key West.

During that summer in 1959, Key West was in the process of significant social and economic change caused by the ousting of Fulgencio Batista, the President/Dictator of Cuba, by Fidel Castro earlier that year. As a result, Cuba was no longer a tourist destination and the Havana Ferry terminal located on Stock Island was permanently closed. At the time, I didn't completely understand the politics or implications of that revolution, but the Gulfstream policy was straightforward and simple: "No Political Discussions" inside the store. Before that policy was enacted, shouting matches and fights would break out inside the market as Batista and Castro sympathizers aired their differences, often resulting in overturned displays and broken glass. These confrontations sometimes spilled out onto White Street resulting in uneasy neighborhood tensions. Castro's Cuba was just too close for comfort, while permeating Key West with mucho discomfort!

Our first customer of the morning arrived nonchalantly on a dilapidated, rusted beach bike. I watched through store front windows pasted with paper signs announcing today's specials as he carefully leaned his bike against a pole just outside the market entrance. Once inside, he greeted Pete with a morning smile and an abbreviated hand wave. I had seen him before in the Gulfstream and the way he carried himself, with a subtle confidence, contrasted with his disheveled appearance. I observed with intent curiosity, as he meandered the tight isles while carefully checking a small paper list. I considered him down on his luck or maybe just another easy-living Key West transient without skills or education.

Finally arriving at the cash register, he conversed with Pete in Cuban while I double bagged his groceries, as he had politely requested. Something about Castro and Cuba, as I picked up a word here and there. After thanking me, he was gone with his bagged groceries struggling to maintain their balance within the bike's front basket.

"Mike, know whose groceries you just bagged?"
"No Pete, I don't."
"Tennessee Williams." Said Pete.
"Who's Tennessee Williams?" I replied.

If I had realized my short comings, I might have caught that 'Streetcar Named Desire' out of town. I had heard of Hank Williams the musician, Tennessee Ernie Ford the singer and Ted Williams the baseball player who often visited Key West to bone fish, but never Tennessee Williams. Pete explained that he was a famous author who lived in Key West and wrote stage plays that were performed on Broadway in New York City. His unshaved, disheveled appearance certainly didn't announce his literary success, but his eccentricity matched my assumptions for an author. I took my chance encounter with Mr. Williams with a grain of salt while I began bagging groceries for another customer. My unrecognized ignorance would eventually be fully realized years later while watching Elizabeth Taylor and Paul Newman in Tennessee William's, 'Cat on a Hot Tin Roof'.

After walking home from Key West High School in early September of that year, I was surprised to see several parked cars near the front entrance of my house. Remembering my mother mentioning that she was hosting a social meeting of Navy wives, I decided to avoid possible introductions and proceed directly to my bedroom to practice guitar. Entering the front door, I quickly glanced into the living room and was shocked to see Mr. Tennessee Williams sitting in the middle of our living floor surrounded by a menagerie of females. He was smiling and enjoying his stage as the center of attention, just like I'm enjoying sharing these memories of our chance encounters. I don't think Tennessee recognized me without my Gulfstream apron!

Sand Key Lighthouse
By Mike

Straddling the bow of our small boat like a hood ornament on a speeding car, the iridescent pastels of submerged corals flash their momentary colors as we traveled towards Sand Key. Three of us, Bobby, Don and myself, all hydroplaning across an endless transparent mirror, reflecting clouds, sky and an infinite atmosphere without distortion.

Spotted Eagle Rays dart from beneath the bow like stealthy flying saucers in what is perceived to be just inches of water due to its liquid lens of crystal clarity. Ballyhoos challenge us to short speed trials as they skip-by with winged fins and vibrating propeller-like tails dipped into the liquid mirror.

As reality begins releasing its gravitational hold, I find myself suddenly alone. The constant drone of the engine seems to disappear along with the horizon. There is no longer delineation between water and sky as I am strangely suspended in an environment with no reference. Just a breathless, weightless reflection flying inches above the mirror in astonished amazement. It is simply incredible!

Suddenly, a bright pinpoint of acetylene light burns a tiny hole in the middle of my imaginary mirror as the Sand Key lighthouse flashes its distant arrival.

"Hey Mike, are you OK up there?"
Turning around, after gathering myself, I responded.
"Yeah, Bobby, I'm fine!"

I was never sure how much time had passed, but it was a perfect day, in a perfect place as reality began to reestablish itself. After Don dropped anchor, we entered the crystal clear waters and were instantly greeted by curious schools of colorful reef fish as several Barracuda watched from a calculated distance. Conch Life on Duval Street* now seemed a little less important, but much more secure, as we are no longer at the top of the food chain. After several hours of meandering through canyons of coral and spearing several large Grouper, it was time to take a break to warm up on the inviting beach sand surrounding Sand Key. Diving below 15 feet (4.5 m) to chase down a Grouper is like entering a frigid shower compared to the warm water surface temperatures surrounding the reef. It's cold down there!

* Duval Street, 1.2 miles in length (1.9 km), connects the Gulf of Mexico with the Caribbean and is the social center of Key West.

Looking up, the Sand Key lighthouse seemed to be tilting towards Havana, some 90 miles (145 km) across the blue abyss, as vertigo pushed me into the warm island sand. We had been snorkeling all morning and feeling the heat penetrate my cold body seemed to bridge a spiritual connection with the universe. It was a moment of pure, relaxing warmth as we lay stretched out on a scintillating virgin surface.

Eventually, the relentless sun forced us into the welcomed shade of the lighthouse column where we wolfed down several sandwiches followed by ice cold sodas. Even though we had snorkeled Sand Key waters many times before, this was the first time tidal sand completely covered the coral key. Cautioned by parents that swimming on a full stomach was asking for trouble, we decided to take time and explore the vacant, but fully functional lighthouse.

The structure was first built in the early 19th century and housed a keeper's residence on an elevated lower deck supported by spider leg scaffolding. Climbing the rusted stairs onto the deck, the visual angle of the water begin to reveal coral heads previously hidden by surface reflection. Approaching the locked entrance, we were greeted by a plaque prohibiting trespassing, as this was the property of the U.S. Coast Guard in 1960. Witnessed by only a few gulls and diving cormorants, the door surprisingly flew open with a single, synchronized push!

Requiring several minutes for our vision to adjust, we eventually viewed the emptiness of the dank vacated living quarters once occupied by a keeper. Noticing several large gas cylinders strapped against a wall, I followed the connected copper tubing across the ceiling and up the lighthouse's central column. Looking up, I could see the flashing light synchronized with the double clicking of a mechanical mechanism. Without much thought, I immediately started towards the light.

"Mike, I wouldn't go up there, it doesn't look safe."
"It's OK Bobby," I replied. "The Coast Guard uses these steps all the time, so they must be safe."
"Don't look directly at the light Mike," Don warned.
"OK, I won't."

The dilapidated staircase protruded from the curved walls like dead limbs from a tree trunk. As I began to ascend the spiral labyrinth, I instinctively reached for the safety of a handrail, which didn't exist! Looking below, my classmates stared back with dimly lit expressions of concern. If a step failed to support my 100 pounds (38 kg), it would be all over. Nevertheless, I was compelled to continue by the adventure of it all.

Reaching the top, I entered into a circular glass enclosure containing a large spherical Fresnel lens which housed a blinding bright gas flame. Two flashes of light, with specified time pauses, would specifically identify Sand Key and warn mariners of the submerged reef below. While moving around the large glass crystal, sun rays showed off their spectrums in dazzling bursts of refracted color. Noticing a small door that opened onto an outside catwalk, I decided to follow my curiosity.

Once outside, the view was breathtaking, as I scanned across an infinite blue horizon towards Cuba, and then back at a faintly visible Key West. One hundred feet below (30.5 m), the transparent reef was now painted with a multitude of water colored pastels revealing characteristics previously unknown to us. Just 100 meters to the north, a large patch of white sand contained the faint outline of an old sunken boat. I couldn't wait to tell the others what I had discovered.

Navigating down the perilous spiraling steps inside the lighthouse column was much more frightening than my recent ascent. As I was previously pulled up by curiosity, now looking down, I began to contemplate what might happen if I slipped and plunged down the shaft pulled by gravity. S*P*L*A*T. Right onto the rusted floor, while waiting friends witnessed my untimely demise. Approaching the bottom, my steps quickened in order to conceal the fear behind a welcoming smile.

Once outside, we carefully repositioned the damaged entry door to look normal and headed back to our boat to explore the outline of the sunken vessel seen from atop the lighthouse. Setting anchor about 50 meters north east of the reef, we splashed into water with a pure white sand bottom. To our surprise, we were hovering above a lifeless desert. Without the protection of the coral, reef fish felt vulnerable to predator attack, and therefore avoided this area altogether.

Excitement rapidly faded into disappointment, as our group hovered weightlessly while scanning the sandy bottom for any hint of a sunken hull. It wasn't long before I found myself as the loan searcher while others meandered off towards the coral reef. I believe it was like trying to find the image of the man-in-the-moon while standing on the moon. Anyway, my credibility was eroding into an incredible fantasy as I continued the search.

After several minutes, I decided to head back and join the others as I could see their snorkel spurts in the distance. Evidently, the ocean currents had separated us more than expected. Not to worry, as I calmly finned my way towards the group, intermittently verifying my position while observing the sandy bottom. Suddenly, I noticed a large Queen Helmet Conch slinking across the sandy sea floor. Wow! This was the largest Queen I had ever seen.

Without remembering that curiosity sometimes abruptly shortened the lives of cats, I continually watched the gargantuan mollusk from the surface while catching my breath. Then with a single burst of energy, I thrusted my body vertical and dove straight towards the Queen, 25 feet (7.5 m) straight down. On the way down, I had to equalize pressure in my ears and mask while managing a spear gun. Grabbing the shell by the helmet rim with both hands, the creature contracted into the safety of its shell as I pushed off the sand bottom. Not immediately noticing that the sun was no longer at full strength, I slowly began ascending to the surface with my prize. This was going to be a good find after all!

As I continued towards the surface, the attenuated sunlight, subconsciously attributed to clouds, was now recognized as the shadow of a very large shark. The monster had to be 4 or 5 times my length and was directly above me! The Queen was no longer a priority and now it was fight or flight! I actually can't remember what I did at that moment. However, I instantly relinquished the Queen, dropped my spear gun and somehow surfaced to breath. I do remember yelling to my friends … "SHARK, SHARK"! "Get out of the water"! Heeding my warning, everyone swam towards the boat and when I finally arrived, pulled me aboard as fast as possible. In between deep breaths, I tried to describe what I had just seen, but as I related the size of the shark, eyes began to roll in disbelief.

"Mike, maybe it was a Manta Ray, sharks don't get that big." Said Don. "No, I know what a Key Manta looks like and this was a very large shark." I replied in desperation to maintain the integrity of my story.

Of course, there's no such thing as a 25 foot shark in the Florida Keys, or so I thought. Once things calmed down, my credibility continued to slide further down the insanity scale as the teasing persisted. Considering myself lucky to be alive, I convinced Bobby to retrieve my spear gun since I wasn't about to provide that creature with a second chance at dinner. Weighing anchor, we headed home with several Grouper and Hog Snappers after another memorable day at Sand Key. There is nothing like a fresh fish dinner after a long day of diving the outer Keys. And besides, my Mom would be all smiles!

Years later, while watching Jacques Cousteau on TV with my sons Mark and Matthew, I finally saw the shark that cast its shadow and raised my blood pressure to the boiling point. It was a 30 foot whale shark, a harmless, ocean wandering filter feeder. Even though I was never in any real danger, curiosity seems to be a universal trait not just confined to humans, cats or Whale Sharks!

Lovely Rita
By Mike

In the late 1950s, Key West was just a sleepy island stop on the way to Havana, Cuba. It was summer, and when I wasn't skin diving, I worked at the Gulfstream, a neighborhood Cuban Market on White Street. I previously worked as a bag boy at Food Fair, the largest grocery store in Key West, but was dismissed for skipping work to snorkel the Marquises Islands with friends. I simply couldn't pass up the opportunity to dive around a sunken World War II ship. Before my employment at Food Fair, I worked at Zeller's Texaco gas station near the Stock Island Bridge. Unfortunately, I was let go for having a little fun squirting water on the mechanic. My past work history notwithstanding, I valued my job at the Gulfstream and was determined not to repeat previous indiscretions. My responsibilities could be summed up as whatever needed to be done: bagging groceries, stocking shelves, pricing product, filling plastic bags with black beans, unloading food trucks, installing front window advertising and sweeping the floor. I had a great job with a welcomed assortment of activities, plus work hours that permitted sufficient time for summer adventures.

Operation Petticoat and PT-109, two block-buster Hollywood movies, were being filmed in Key West around that time and it was always good public relations for movie actors and crew to visit local establishments. Well, one couldn't get more local than the Gulfstream Market which was owned by Mr. Munos with a clientele ranging from the Mayor of Key West to the local Cuban and Conch residents. I never got to meet Cary Grant and Tony Curtis since most of their scenes were filmed back in Hollywood, but there were 'store-stopping' moments when all those Operation Petticoat Nurses paraded through the Gulfstream in short shorts, then lining up for me to bag their groceries. These girls were dripping with back-seat excitement, if you know what I mean, and it was difficult not to stare where a teenage boy shouldn't.

When Cliff Robertson, Ty Hardin and the PT-109 movie crew visited the Gulfstream things were just as exciting, but for different reasons. No beautiful girls to entice my youthful desires, but watching several female shoppers melt in the aisles due to a star-struck overload was visually entertaining. Unknown to my fellow employees, I had already met Mr. Clyde Howdy, a supporting actor and stunt man who was staying at the Holiday Inn near my home. Several months prior I had purchased my first guitar, and not long afterwards, encountered Mr. Howdy playing *The Whiffenpoof Song* while relaxing outside his room. I introduced myself as a fellow guitar player, which was a bit of a stretch, but he took me under his musical wing anyway. At that time, I knew a total of 4 chords in the key of C, and was intensely intrigued on how he played melody with chords. Many years later, I eventually learned to play *The Whiffenpoof Song* just like Clyde. When Mr. Howdy finally finished loading his grocery cart and approached Pete, the cashier at the check-out stand where I was also working as a bag boy, he said;

"Hi Mike, I didn't know you worked here at the Gulfstream."

Suddenly, my social status went soaring into the stratosphere. To be recognized by a movie star was the ultimate kudos!

Of course, movie star stopovers at the Gulfstream Market was not an everyday occurrence. It only happened twice during my employment, but those were, and still are, exciting memorable moments. Normal Gulfstream days were relatively slow compared to the Food Fair Market where I use to work, but a multitude of different tasks would keep me thoroughly occupied throughout the day. During the early afternoons when the market was the busiest, I would often help Pete at the cash register bag groceries to eliminate long customer lines. While assisting Pete, sometimes I had moments between customers to relax, look around the market and observe Gulfstream shoppers, most of whom I recognized as return customers. Every once and a while, there was this one very attractive, petite female customer who would catch me looking at her with overheated eyes that shouldn't have been looking. I was 16, overloaded with youth, and she was a customer in her 40s. It was embarrassing as my eyes tried to casually disengage, but she was just as attractive as those Operation Petticoat nurses. While bagging her groceries, I found myself in uncharted waters trying to socially navigate without a compass. My silence was deafening, but she always thanked me before exiting the market. I had a similar experience in the past where I was infatuated by my twenty something year old Art Teacher, Miss Stathopoulos. She was a Greek Goddess who was not only a great teacher, but who I secretly fell in love with, as did most of my 7th grade male classmates. Looking back at these adolescent desires across my life, I have come to realize that it is just part of growing up, but all attractions and past loves eventually migrate to a special place inside one's heart to peacefully reside to provide reflective comfort.

I can't remember how Paul and I met that summer, most likely through common friends. He attended a private school in Miami and was home until the fall. Paul was a little on the wild side, which was socially accepted as a condition possibly associated with private school antics. One Saturday, Paul, Bobby and I agreed to meet outside Kress's Department Store in downtown Key West before going to see an afternoon movie. After waiting a while, we were certain that Paul was a no show and decided to get in line for the movie. Just as we began to walk away towards the Monroe Theater, there was a heavy thump from inside one of Kress's large plate glass windows. It was Paul, who was posing as a store mannequin inside the display window! Nonetheless, Paul and I enjoyed snorkeling Woman's Key, attending Friday night teen dances at the Elks Club and playing pin ball games at arcades on Duval Street. In a few years, Paul and I would be housemates while attending Junior College in St. Petersburg, Florida. I could easily write another book of short stories about that experience as many of my Key West High School classmates also attend that college. Socially, I was having the time of my life in St. Pete at the expense of academic success.

Paul and I became close friends during that summer in 1959, and one day he invited me over to his house for dinner. Paul's dad was a reputable Monroe County attorney and lived in the best section of Key West. My mother was well aware of the family's Key West social status and began preparing me by emphasizing how to eat with manners and to start with the outside utensils and work your way in as the dinner unfolds. I soon began to consider the possibility of my mother's version of reality. Maybe this was not just an ordinary dinner since she had extensive experience with Navy Officer dining protocols. I became a bit nervous not knowing what to expect.

After passing my mother's inspection as properly dressed, I took a city bus over to Paul's neighborhood near Southard Street. I made my way past several well-kept grand homes of the past century, finally arriving at my destination. Paul's home was simply majestic! I was standing in front of a very large white Victorian home, secluded by mature tropical plants and surrounded by a white picket fence with a wrought iron entry gate. How I originally envisioned Paul's family home and the real estate reality I was about to enter were totally incompatible. After rechecking the address, I opened the gate and cautiously ascended the front porch steps onto an impressive front porch with wicker chairs and colorful hanging fuchsia plants suspended above arched railings. Peering through windows with stained glass perimeters, I could see several well-dressed gentlemen engaged in animated conversation. Maybe my mother was correct, this was not going to be an ordinary dinner.

After knocking, I was greeted by Paul and invited into a stately sitting room where his dad, dressed in a white linen suit, along with several attorneys were smoking Cuban cigars and sipping straight whiskey. It was a scene right out of a Bogart movie as I struggled with my greeting lines after Paul's introduction. Paul's dad was in the process of welcoming me into his home, when suddenly a lovely female voice filled the room with,

"Well, this is Mike. It's so nice to finally meet you."

Turning to greet that voice, our eyes instantly locked in startling astonishment and there was no looking away this time as I had previously done while observing her shopping at the Gulfstream. I was trapped in a terrible, very embarrassing nightmare moment with no escape.

"Mike, this is my mom, Rita," said Paul.

Rita smiled with the confidence of age, and asked me if I wanted something to drink. I must have nodded yes, and obediently followed her into the kitchen. She suddenly stopped, held my hand, and then gave me the wonderful hug I had always imagined.

"Mike, it's OK," said Rita. "It's just going to be our little secret."

Eventually, I confessed almost all, but not everything, to Paul who referred to his mom as "Lovely Rita".

I can't remember much about that evening or even what was served for dinner, but over that summer I was a frequent guest at their home and eventually "Lovely Rita" just became Paul's mom. One day, while bagging her groceries, the owner of the Gulfstream stopped to say hello. After their short conversation, she stated to Mr. Munos that I always bagged her groceries with extra care and awarded me with a comforting hug before departing with a smile!

A feeling of belonging that had been missing since my childhood was beginning to take root in Key West. I finally felt accepted within a caring Conch community. I was no longer just another Navy Brat!

Armed With Words
By Mike

Dr. Campbell often greeted students, while checking for acceptable attire, as we entered Key West High School at the main Flagler Street entrance in the late 1950s. A stern, but friendly Principal who believed in following and enforcing the rules. Many girls were sent home for revealing too much loveliness, and for guys, a neat appearance was required with combed hair and T-shirts void of cigarette packs secured in a rolled up sleeve. Our dress code was relatively relaxed, but once a fashion boundary was crossed, entry was denied until corrected. A wooden paddle supposedly hung in his office ready to impose corrective action for conduct unbecoming a student. Fortunately, I never found myself on the receiving end of that rumored device.

My favorite subjects were rooted in the sciences, even though I had problems with algebra. I procrastinated many difficult assignments until the very last moment for reasons I still don't understand today. Looking back,

I was most likely dyslectic since reading was so challenging that I often fell asleep on page one. Plus, my spelling was absolutely atrocious. Some adults politely labeled me as a slow learner, but that phrase could also be considered a euphemism for a low IQ. Whatever the cause, I found it much easier to play guitar rather than subjecting myself to the rigors of the required reading to obtain passing grades.

Mr. Conner's English IV Class was a contradiction in that I really liked the man, but just shunned the subject. My goal was to simply attain a passing grade by any means possible, thus avoiding the wrath of my authoritarian father who always presented himself as a straight "A" student. English IV was essentially a composition class with hours of required reading and writing. Therefore, for me, a major problem. During the first week of class, Mr. Conner explained that our Senior English Class would read 'Great Expectations' by Charles Dickens focusing on character development and story analysis. I really had no clue what he was talking about, but when he held that dictionary size novel up for the class to view, I instantly knew I was in trouble, even from my seat in the back row. On prior book-report assignments, I readily relied upon book summaries published in Reader's Digest to circumvent my struggles with reading. However, 'Great Expectations' was a literary classic with no book review available, at least not to me. My plan was to pay particular attention in class and pray for the best possible outcome.

Every Monday, Mr. Conner assigned twenty spelling words from the Scholastic Aptitude Test (SAT) book which all students were required to purchase in preparation for that dreaded college entrance exam. Obtaining good grades on these weekly spelling tests was paramount in helping me secure a passing grade in English IV. On one particular week, the words were especially eccentric and probably rooted in the Ancient Greek lexicon. Procrastinating to the very last moment, I decided to hastily scribble most of the words on the inside of my lower left forearm just before entering the classroom. Of course most would consider this as Grade 'A' cheating, but in my case it was just survival of the fittest. Sometimes desperation conceals the consequences of wearing a short sleeve shirt.

During the test, I honestly attempted to spell the words from memory, but eventually I had to sneak a peek at "the arm" to obtain a passing grade. Mr. Conner, like all teachers during a test, would monitor the class from his desk at the front of the classroom or slowly meander the class perimeter to make sure our test ethics were intact. I was keenly aware of his monitoring habits and very careful not to be too obvious while glancing at my arm, but multitasking under pressure can be a dangerous activity. Suddenly, Mr. Conner grabbed my arm from behind and yanked me out of my seat! I was now S*H*O*C*K*I*N*G*L*Y the center of attention.

"We have a cheater among us and I have caught him red-handed!" Mr. Conner proclaimed, as he pulled me to the front of the class.

This was beyond embarrassing and I felt like a cat, helplessly held by the scruff of the neck, before being tossed out the door. I knew instantly, I was now going to be sent to Dr. Campbell's office and would most likely end up on the receiving end of his alleged corrective action implement of pain. Then, suddenly looking closely at my arm, Mr. Conner abruptly broke out in laughter.

"On second thought Mr. Kohut, you can return to your seat and finish the test. The words on your arm are misspelled!"

Now the real embarrassment was about to become a reality, I couldn't even cheat correctly!

However, on second thought, what a welcomed relief! Not only had I simultaneously escaped Dr. Campbell's corrective action, but also the wrath of my dad. My day was positively improving, spelling test failure, notwithstanding.

From that day forward, I abandoned my dishonest 'Grade A' cheating and thankfully received a passing grade in English IV as my attitude began to change. I never did read Great Expectations, but I did follow class discussions with renewed interest. Mr. Conner never treated me differently from any other student and that embarrassing incident was never mentioned or referred to during the remainder of the semester. I think he knew that my ethical center was reestablished by self-correcting embarrassment. Just like I am enjoying writing this story, I know Mr. Conner has experienced similar enjoyment while recalling my cheating heart. That realization set the stage for whom I would eventually become as an adult ... easy going, truthful, and most of all, empathetic to misguided decisions that precipitate unplanned results.

Later during summer vacation I was listening to KWIZ where Mr. Conner hosted a jazz radio program. He would often spin 'Take Five' by The Dave Brubeck Quartet, still one of my favorite recordings. During a music break, he mentioned that one of his students had a run in with a 25 foot shark out at Sand Key. Well that student was me! So I immediately walked across the Stock Island Bridge and was at the station within ten minutes. He interviewed me on the air and I felt that he actually believed my unbelievable encounter. However, my Conch companions were not easily convinced and possibly remain so to this day! Nonetheless, it's my story and I'm sticking to it!

I joined the Marine Corps in 1964 and entered USMC Electronics School in San Diego, California with intact academic ethics. After my four year hitch in the Corps was up, I entered College with the same ethics since I now held myself to excessively high academic standards. During my very last final exam before graduating from the California State University at Long Beach with a BS in Medical Microbiology, I was struggling with a difficult Bacterial Physiology question. Suddenly, another student's test paper floated onto the floor after being dislodged from her desk by a sudden burst of wind from an opened window. As I glanced down, the answer was delivered.

I smiled, was it from the Devil or God?

In The Still of The Night
By Mike

After extinguishing all lights, we slowly coasted to a dead stop in front of her house sometime after midnight. The night was softly quiet with the entire neighborhood smothered in sleep. Carefully exiting the black 1953 Chevy in stealthy silence, I huddled near the vehicle's trunk with nervous apprehension.

Several hours earlier we were all just riding around Key West looking for something to do. Michael, sitting in the front passenger's seat, turned around clutching a can of beer and asked if I was 'turned on' by that skinny freshman girl with horned rimmed glasses. I instantly knew who he was talking about. In my mind, Donna wasn't that skinny, just a slightly slim girl who took exceptional pride in her dress and appearance.

"You mean Donna?" I replied.
"Yeah Mike, we heard that she has the hots for you."

I should have been elated, since I was unaware of being the heartthrob of anyone at Key West High School in 1960. Even though Donna's bloom into feminine adolescence was just beginning, I often took note of her unfolding sensuality when we passed in the halls between classes. I just couldn't recall any noteworthy or inviting eye contact emanating from behind those conspicuous eye glasses that always seemed to divert one's attention away from her subtle, but lovely features. Even though I was attracted to Donna, I perceived her as academically superior, and therefore decided to move on towards less challenging pursuits of the heart. I simply had little confidence when it came to exposing my heart and below average grades to possible rejection.

To avoid embarrassment and social taunting as we drove with no particular destination in mind, I responded with a big peer pressure little white lie!

"I wouldn't touch her with a 10 foot pole."
"OK Mike, if that's the case, why don't you give her a fish!" Said Joe.
"Look, I don't even know where she lives," I replied.

As my words were being aired, I instantly knew what was coming.

"I know where she lives," Bill replied!
"OK, that settles it. Let's get a trash canned Tarpon from the harbor so you can give it to her Mike." Joe declared.
Turning the car around, we now had a definite destination; the sport fishing docks at Garrison Bight Marina along N. Roosevelt Boulevard.

Passing around the last can of beer previously procured for us by a sailor on Duval Street, our destination was finalized, even without my verbal approval. Not knowing what I had gotten myself into, it was now out of my control as I felt kidnapped by my back seat words.

Key West has some crazy traditions, and giving someone a fish is one of the most revered. Receiving a fish in your front yard could be from a close friend, a rival or some social statement that needs to be aired via the smelly deposit. In any case, the fish represents a message from someone you may know. It's a stinky declaration of one sort or another!

Slowly opening the car's trunk as not to make a sound, I grabbed the four foot (1.2 m) Tarpon by its lifeless gills and slid the rigid silver-scaled creature over the bumper and onto the ground with a thud.

It must have weighed over 30 pounds (13.6 kg). After dragging the carcass onto Donna's front lawn, I said,

"OK, let's get the hell out of here!"
"Not yet," someone said.
"Let's put it on her front porch!"

Since I didn't have the strength or inclination to pick up the slimy remains, Bill wrapped the fish's tail in a discarded towel from the trunk and began spinning it around like an Olympic Athlete competing in the Hammer Throw. Bill was a weight lifter and after totally misjudging his strength along with the creature's centrifugal energy, he finally released the putrid projectile into the still of the night.

In slow motion, we watched the fish fly across the front lawn, over Donna's front porch banister, and come to rest in her parent's living room after - S*M*A*S*H*I*N*G - through a large plate glass window! Frozen in astonishment, we quickly thawed and sped off into the eyes of the night! Parking in a grove of coconut palms adjacent to Smathers Beach to calm our nerves, we swore ourselves to absolute secrecy under a full moon. By never mentioning our dreadful deed to anyone, we would avoid social embarrassment, suspension from high school, parental restriction and financial repercussions to replace the window. After agreeing, Joe drove us all home in reflective silence.

On Monday morning, while passing by Donna at school, she seemed absolutely normal. There was no indication that suggested something terrible happened over the weekend, nor was there any hint of me being her heart throb which had pushed this whole incident forward in the first place. Bill, Michael and Joe also agreed that she appeared unaffected by our misguided prank. We all decided that Donna must be silently listening for fish story gossip to surface so she could follow the smelly trail and reel in the slimy culprits. As time passed, we religiously adhered to our midnight promise before the Dark Angel to remain mute, but the eyes of that night have never closed and to this day continue to wait for peaceful sleep.

After graduation, we all went our separate ways into life, but the fish incident has always been quietly smoldering somewhere inside my soul. And besides, I have always asked the question; did we actually have Donna's correct address? Maybe we had the wrong house! In that case, what unfortunate family was on the receiving end of our night shattering flying fish?

Now some 60 plus years later, I have decided to unmute the past so those eyes can finally close and attempt to catch up on some well-deserved sleep. It took a while for me to recognize the dangers of imagined social pressures and the balance between the consequence of words, actions and self-esteem. I cannot undo the past, but I have moved forward as a better person ... not perfect, but better!

A Science Fair Blast
By Mike

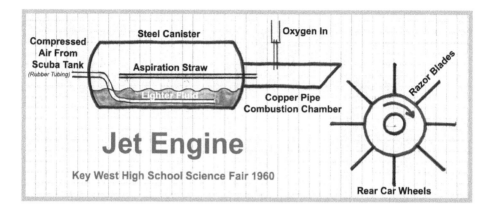

Compressed Air From Scuba Tank *(Rubber Tubing)* — Steel Canister — Oxygen In — Aspiration Straw — Lighter Fluid — Copper Pipe Combustion Chamber — Razor Blades

Jet Engine

Key West High School Science Fair 1960

Rear Car Wheels

Since my Key West High School 11th Grade Science Fair project was due on Monday morning with judging in the early afternoon, I needed to create my required project over the weekend; in just 3 short days! Mr. Ekelund, my physics teacher, informed our class of this project several months ago, but it was always pushed onto the back burner until now; it was a do-or-die situation! The most difficult part was deciding what to do and decision time had suddenly arrived. I had always loved science, but I needed a project that would authenticate that love with a 1st Place Ribbon. Then, out of the blue, it suddenly came to me on Saturday morning ... I would build a jet powered car. Wow!

OK, it wasn't going to be a real jet car, but rather a miniature working demo. The exhaust from a jet engine could easily turn a car's rear wheels, similar to how the wind turns the blades of a windmill. It would be a great project, guaranteed to get me an A+ and peer group recognition. Maybe even win a scholarship or medal of some sort.

HYPOTHESIS: A jet engine could be used to power a car.

MATERIALS: I spent most of Saturday gathering the following materials:

Materials	Purpose
Steel Insecticide Canister	Jet Engine
Copper Pipe	Combustion Chamber
Wood Cradle	Jet Engine Horizontal Support
Scuba Tank	Compressed Air
Lighter Fluid	Propellant Fuel
Rubber Tubing	Compressed Air Injection
Spool & Razor Blades	Impeller
Rear Wheels & Axel	Car Parts
Poster	Diagram & Explanation

CONSTRUCTION: The filling plug and spray nozzle of an emptied *Steel Insecticide Canister* were removed and set aside. The *Internal Aspiration Straw* attached to the spray nozzle port was needed, so allowed to remain. A 15 cm length of *Copper Pipe* was selected to securely mate with the external spray nozzle port to be used as the *Combustion Chamber*. The other end of the copper pipe was cut at a 45 degree angle to simulate a jet fighter's exhaust. The engine was cradled in a wooden stand designed to hold the jet canister horizontal during the demo.

METHOD: The 12 cm diameter *Steel Canister* is filled with 50 mL of the Propellant Fuel (*Lighter Fluid*) and cradled to maintain a horizontal position. This small volume of fuel will assure that the *Internal Aspiration Straw* stays well above the liquid fuel. One end of a long segment of *Rubber Tubing* is inserted into the filling port until submerged into the *Lighter Fluid*. The other end of the tubing is connected to the *Scuba Tank's* air valve to provide compressed air. As the *Compressed Air* enters the canister, the lighter fluid is agitated forming flammable fumes which are forced through the *Internal Aspiration Straw* and into the *Combustion Chamber*. Once the fumes are ignited in the combustion chamber, the jet engine will start. The jet exhaust then impels the *Razor Blades* which are securely attached to a rotatable spindle serving as the car's axle, forcing the wheels to rotate.

INITIAL RESULTS: Regrettably, it didn't work. The jet engine's exhaust resembled a feeble Bunsen Burner flame with insufficient force to even reach the rear wheels. My project was dead, and ... no Nobel Prize for Science. But, wait!

REVELATION: Why not inject oxygen into the *Combustion Chamber* by drilling a small hole into the *Copper Pipe* and inserting a basketball air inflation needle to deliver the oxygen? I suddenly realized that Mr. Lazier's Chemistry Class has saved the day. A second section of tubing could then be connected between the needle and an oxygen bottle to create the force needed to turn the wheels. My project was alive and well! My Dad was a Navy MD and had a small compressed canister of oxygen in his bedroom for emergency use due to his chronic heart disease. Dad always went to work early, so it would be easy to borrow a little oxygen for my project. He would be extremely proud of my 1st Place ribbon!

CONCLUSION: Working past my bedtime on Sunday, I managed to finish my project poster just before Mom declared, lights out. Although it was impossible to test the new oxygen injection system, I confidently fell asleep wrapped in a warm Key West breeze. Sweet dreams of jet powered wheels and science awards were just behind closed eyes.

Monday morning started with the usual breakfast chaos, packing lunches and getting four kids ready for school. My Mom performed her daily magic with the experience of being the oldest sibling in a family of eleven! I had to scramble that morning, assembling and packing my science project for the bus ride to Key West High School. The smuggled oxygen tank hid in plain sight as I waved good-bye to Mom, after being assured with a hug that everything would be fine. Making my way to the bus stop with a back-slung scuba tank, unruly poster and a heavy box of hardware was probably not that unusual in Key West. After all, members of the girl's rifle team were allowed to transport their rifles on a city bus. Sometimes those gun-toting females were dropped off at the dairy queen for an armed treat.

Arriving at school, I found myself guided into the gymnasium along with other potential Nobel laureates to begin setting up our projects. Mr. Ekelund informed us that this year we would be judged by professors from the University of Miami. In other words, we should be prepared for questions from real scientists.

Each project was assigned a small table arranged in a series of parallel rows. After fueling the jet canister with lighter fluid and connecting compressed air and oxygen tubing, my jet powered car was ready to go. Stepping back to admire the future of automotive transportation, I noticed a cute blonde carefully positioning delicate toothpick crystals, covered in colorful cellophane, on an adjacent table. Taking a moment to scan other rows, I was relieved that no one else had a jet engine. I would be in a category all by myself.

To make sure the jet was operational, I opened the valve on my scuba tank to apply compressed air to the canister. As I was about to light the combustion chamber, Mr. Ekelund announced that our projects looked good and that we should all go to our 2nd period classes. Unable to test the oxygen injection system, I closed the air valve and left the gymnasium. I was unsure how much oxygen would be needed to turn the jet car's wheels in order to impress the judges, but I was confident that the oxygen valve could be easily adjusted.

After lunch we were instructed to stand by our projects and quietly wait for the judges. I was nervously contemplating how I would explain my jet engine when the cute blonde began describing her crystals to the judges. Evidently, she did a great job as they shook her hand and began walking my way.

Assembling in front of my project and without a word, the judges began reading my poster. Instinctively, I moved out of the way so they could observe my masterpiece. Then, one judge asked,

"What kind of a jet engine did you build?"
"I'm not sure, but this jet uses compressed air and lighter fluid," I responded.
"You have RAM Jet. Please tell us how it operates," the judge requested.

I began with details of how air from the scuba tank creates fuel vapor that ignites in the combustion chamber, powering the wheels of the car. Reaching under the table, I opened the scuba tank's air valve and after a few seconds lit the end of the combustion chamber with a match.

As before, an unimpressive, feeble flame emerged from the combustion chamber similar to that of a kerosene lantern. Reaching under the table again, I opened the oxygen valve and said,

"Now let's inject a little oxygen to see what happens!"

After a delay of a few seconds, a single jet flame blasted out of the combustion chamber with the sound of a shotgun! The jet fired 2 or 3 times a second at first, but rapidly intensified into a continuous combustion chamber roar of a jet plane getting ready to takeoff. Before, I could shut off the oxygen, my jet did what jets do ... it became a projectile and flew from my table!

All three judges hit the floor fearing for their lives and that cute blonde's toothpick crystals were blown to smithereens. Thank goodness her project was already judged. The jet engine laid lifeless, disconnected from air and oxygen tubing, at the far end of the gymnasium floor. The rear wheels of the car were never found, and fortunately, no one was actually injured with the exception of my pride. Astonished and startled in the moments that followed, I knew that my Nobel Prize and associated accolades were long gone. My memory of other events that followed that day have become foggy over the years, but my final project grade was a disappointing D+. "D" for Dangerous and "+" for supervision required!

The very next year, a few days before the science fair, my best friend Bobby asked if he could use my Jet Engine poster as his project. Procrastinators seem to hang out with other procrastinators! Bobby received a "B" grade for his explanation of my jet powered car without an actual working model.

Life is not fair, as I have rediscovered many times, but it should be fun!

Although my imaginary Nobel Prize for Science never came to fruition, I know I'm anonymously famous, maybe even infamous, in the hallowed halls of science at University of Miami.

Smooth As Silk
By Mike

The Blue

Snorkeling for Grouper and Snapper, Don, Bobby and I weightlessly navigate the coral canyons off Sand Key, a small patch of sand with a lighthouse situated on the edge of the 90 mile abyss separating Key West from Cuba. Schools of brightly colored reef fish greet us in tightly packed clusters, but give way in synchronized dance as we approach in search of our prey. Snapper seems to navigate the coral heads with calculated caution as we approach, while grouper hug the coral crevasses near the sea floor seeking potential hiding places. Snapper have empty eyes as often seen displayed on crushed ice in a fish market, but grouper have eyes like canines which seem to connect and communicate feelings. After several missed spear shots at a tasty ten pound grouper, looking up with connected eyes just before vanishing into the coral, I could almost hear that fish say,

"No way am I joining you guys for dinner!"

Never totally ignoring the on-looking pack of twenty to thirty silver barracuda flashing their sharp spiculated teeth while encircling us like an ominous living wreath, we simply view them as spineless spectators in a vast underwater stadium. An abrupt charge with a pointed spear gun ends intermittent barracuda curiosity, as they always retreat back down to the safety of the spectator pack. Barracuda are like pigeons on city streets, they are always expected inhabitants of the reef.

We are snorkeling on the edge of the reef which plunges into a cold, dark blue abyss deeper than the Grand Canyon. Never having the courage or curiosity to venture out there, we hug the safety of the coral, just like the fish. The Blue is visually a lifeless void compared to the plentiful fish and colorful coral on the reef, yet demanding of our attention with imagined anxiety of what scaly predator might emerge from the deep. Looking into the Blue is like searching an endless blue sky without clouds, birds or kites. There is nothing to focus upon, so you intermittently search for movement between penetrating shafts of refracted sun light to maintain vigilance.

After several missed spear-gun shots, the fish have finally figured out our intentions; the hunt in this area of the reef is over as our prey have scattered or have taken defensive positions within the safety of the coral. While snorkeling to a different location to continue hunting for a fresh fish dinner, my peripheral vision detects a disturbance in the Blue. Scanning the open ocean for any slight movement, I suddenly focus on something emerging out of the azure haze. Approaching at high speed, three Lemon Sharks fly by in perfect Blue Angel formation. Instinctively, the three of us snap together like released rubber bands into a sea urchin posture with spear-guns pointing outward for protection. Realizing that escape is impossible without becoming live bait, we wait with a calm anxiety to assess our best option for survival. Subconsciously, that other person inside of my brain began readjusting the limits to my youthful definition of immortality.

During their second flyby, this time within inches, I instinctively push hard against the ten foot prehistoric body with my free hand. Startled by my unplanned and probably unexpected physical contact, the stealthy three accelerate back into the Blue to reassess our aggression. Frozen in our defensive positions we scan the open ocean with a wait-and-see defiance. Reconsidering our situation, in instantaneous and speechless coordination, we individually arrived at the same decision. With our escape now at hand, we frantically unravel our sea urchin posture and power swim back to our anchored boat, 50 bloodcurdling meters away.

Splashing into the safety of our craft, Don immediately starts the engine to assure our safety. After Bobby recovered the anchor, we all started laughing to hide what could have been a sad story for our parents, classmates and especially us.

Although there would be no fresh fish dinner, we enjoyed a very peaceful ride back to Key West as the sun and warm wind evaporated salt water from our tanned bodies. Not to arrive home empty handed, we decided to stop and gig a few Langusta before arriving at the Naval Hospital docks near the Stock Island Bridge. It was good to be safely home just in time to witness another breathtaking Key West sunset!

That day at Sand Key has never totally vanished from my memory, but was put aside to reflect upon across time. Being the hunted rather than the hunter is a life changing experience. There was never any panic, just three Key West kids in the process of growing up in our underwater backyard with instincts summoned from ancestral DNA. I can still feel the silky smoothness of that shark's powerful body when it slid beneath the palm of my outstretched hand, as it jetted back into the Blue.

Years later, while attending my 50th Key West High School reunion, we had lunch with several of my classmates at a local Cuban restaurant near the Gulfstream Market where I used to work as a teenager: Bobby Pazo, Jack Sweeting, Ray Gutierrez and David Perez. All three were 3rd generation Key West Conchs. In other words, my wife Kathie and I were having lunch with classmates who grew up on the reefs and who were overflowing with diving experiences and Key West history.

My run-of-the-mill little shark story wasn't even given a second thought by these Conchs who served their Community & Country with distinction!

Bobby Pazo: US Army, Professional Baseball, Professional Guitar

Ray Gutierrez: USMC, Viet Nam Vet, Professional Farrier

David Perez: US Army, Viet Nam Vet, CIA, Professional Treasure Diver

Jack Sweeting: USAF, Construction Business Owner, Philanthropy

Mike Kohut: USMC, Viet Nam Vet, Fresh Water Conch

Bobby Pazo   Ray Gutierrez   David Perez   Jack Sweeting   Mike Kohut
Lunch at El Siboney in Cayo Hueso, June 17th, 2016

Crossing Bridges
By Mike

Seven Mile
Bridge

M r. Munos, my employer and owner of the Gulfstream Market in Key West, was in the process of replacing several freezer units in the summer of 1962 when the backup unit also began to fail. It was quickly decided, before the market opened that morning, that an employee with truck driving experience should travel to Miami and return with a rented refrigeration truck before days end.

Without much thought, I immediately volunteered, mainly to avoid the monotony of restocking shelves, sweeping floors and unloading a waiting truck with heavy boxes of canned goods. Plus, the perceived excitement of travel was just too much to turn down. After informing the manager that I once drove a small pizza truck, it was agreed that I should immediately board the next Greyhound bus out of the Keys. Not stating that I only drove that truck for one day and had no valid driver's license, didn't seem that important at the time, and besides, I was never asked! I was 19, on my own without family support and living in an $11 per week room at the Southern Cross Hotel on Duval Street. I barely made $40.00 per week before taxes. Unfortunately, after food, rent and personal items, there was no cash for beer, movies or chasing girls. Unknown to me at that time, I was in the beginning stages of finally growing up!

A year ago, in January 1961, my dad had a major cardiac event in the middle of my senior year resulting in his abrupt retirement from the Navy after 29 years of service. Consequently, my family relocated to State College, Pennsylvania and arrangements were made for me to stay in Key West with another family to complete my final high school semester. Immediately following class graduation and after turning in my ceremonial robe, I piled into a car with my host family and grudgingly departed Key West to join my family in State College. I never had the chance to celebrate graduation with my classmates, and elimination of that rite-of-passage does not sit well with me even after all this time. My host family was exceedingly nice during my stay and I was always treated as an equal member of their family, but no explanation was ever provided for our abrupt departure. As we traversed Seven Mile Bridge in the middle of that night, I struggled to imprint my memory with the unique environment I had taken for granted over the years. I was leaving what I felt was my only true home, where I had set down deep roots. With darkness in my heart and tears in my eyes, I silently said goodbye to my friends and cursed my life as a Navy Brat. Deep inside I always knew it would end this way, but I pushed back this time and vowed to return to Key West to be with my Conch friends.

I entered Penn State University in the fall of 1961 as a Special Student, a classification designed to give locals a chance to attend a prestigious school in their own backyard. To make a short story even shorter, I really tried to succeed, but was just academically unprepared. However, on a social level, I was having the time of my life playing guitar in pickup bands and staying out to all hours of the night. Key West was beginning to fade a bit, but when asked where I was from, I always sad with pride, Key West! Eventually, my late night carousing and academic implosion was just too much for my dad. Just after the Christmas holidays I found myself standing on a corner in State College during a snow storm with a suitcase-sign that said Key West. I was on my way into a new life to reunite with friends and get my old job back at the Gulfstream Market.

After boarding the Greyhound bus in downtown Key West, I enjoyed a relaxing morning while traveling towards Miami on the Overseas Highway freed from my daily store duties. Spectacular panoramas of small islands seemingly floating on the ocean's distant horizon under a bright blue sky dotted with mid-morning white clouds was reminiscent of many previous travels to attend High School football games on the mainland. Intermittently, the riveting flash of opposing traffic would abruptly interrupt my meanderings, especially while crossing Seven Mile Bridge, a two lane highway barely wide enough for two cars. The fact that I would be driving a truck across this narrow strip of cement in a few hours had not yet registered. I was simply enjoying my unanticipated mini holiday along with relaxing thoughts of my past life.

Once the bus crossed the bridge onto Key Largo, I decided to examine my forged New York Driver's License for any signs of obvious alteration. Opening my wallet, I carefully removed and unfolded the two inch square paper document. In 1962, a driver's license was little more than a postcard size document with an official government stamp, and very easy to alter. I found the license in a gym locker while attending Penn State and meticulously altered the personal information to gain entrance into college bars. It was a magnificent work of art!

After arriving in Miami, I took a cab to the truck rental agency and presented my license upon request. It was closely scrutinized, but eventually accepted, most likely because the truck rental was prepaid. After signing documents, I was led to the waiting vehicle where my preconceived perception of a small refrigeration truck was abruptly shattered. Viewing the 40 foot monster of a truck with a dash board resembling an aircraft's cockpit and a flock of manual gears, my confidence began to wane! Thinking quickly, I asked for cockpit instructions before attempting to negotiate the city streets of downtown Miami.

After a few sporadic, gear-shifting laps around the rental lot, I cautiously exited the establishment only to abruptly stall the truck in the middle of a busy intersection. Ignoring the blast of horns and flashing middle fingers, I was on my way into the unknown. As I began to adjust to my new reality, there was no time to reflect or contemplate anything; downtown Miami was just ahead. About to experience the consequences of self-misrepresentation, I shift the truck into 3rd with a grind of gears. I had no driver's license, little driving experience and was up to my eyeballs in anxiety. Let's be clear, I alone set the stage for Act 1, Scene 1 and my theatrical nightmare was about to begin.

Navigating the traffic swarm in downtown Miami required exceptional concentration. I was fully engulfed in erratic midday traffic eager to cut me off at every chance. After several blocks, I finally eyed the Highway 1 sign to the Keys and signaled to move into the right lane. Although my desperate intentions were being totally ignored, I began bullying the truck to the right and they seemed to get the message ... yield or else! Without fully realizing the truck's large turning radius, the right back wheel suddenly jumped the curb dislodging a corner mailbox from its sidewalk mooring. While observing the shock of astonished pedestrians in my side-mirror, traffic instantly reacted by repelling away from the crazy driver and misbehaving truck. Pretending as if nothing had happened, I continued my wild ride towards Key West.

Once back on the Overseas Highway and travelling through the Keys, my anxiety had somewhat diminished as everything seemed to finally be under control. However, Seven Mile Bridge was just ahead. Little more than a long narrow strip of cement stretching across the open ocean, this passage would be the ultimate test of both nerves and my rookie driving abilities.

Arriving on the notorious bridge with only one exit at Pigeon Key, opposing traffic was thankfully minimal. Nevertheless, I felt very apprehensive as several cars flew by, seemingly almost sideswiping the truck. Eventually, I spied a very large vehicle approaching in the distance. At first, it was no larger than a windshield speck, but in anticipation of its arrival, I began positioning the truck to the far right. As the speck's resolution increased, it slowly morphed into a Greyhound Bus and heart pounding panic began to set in! While burning tire rubber against the bridge's cement abutment, the bus shot by with a startling blast of pressure. That was the salient moment of my regretful holiday. After exiting the bridge, I pulled off the highway on Big Pine Key to recover, wipe sweat, smoke a cigarette and regain my composure.

Pulling up in front of the Gulfstream Market an hour later, I was relieved that the ordeal was over. Mr. Munos came out to greet me and asked if I would back the truck down a tight alley to the loading dock. Still suffering from bridge shock, but without any preconceived consequences of failure, I simply backed the truck using the side mirrors and perfectly positioned it at the dock on the first try.

"Mike, you really do know how to drive a truck, Thank you," said Mr. Munos.

With my mini holiday finally over, I gladly returned to the relatively relaxing duties of market work! Looking back, sometimes life just works out as expected when the probability of failure is exceedingly high. Amen!

I acquired my first valid driver's license five years later in 1967 at the age of 24 after serving in Viet Nam with the 11th Marines. Driving my British Racing Green MGB to the Department of Motor Vehicles in San Bernardino, California for my driver's test, I parked out of sight of the staff to avoid scrutiny. I passed my written driver's test on the first try with no errors, but before taking the road test, the examiner asked:

"Who drove the car to the DMV?"
"My friend," I said, as I looked around to find my imaginary driver.
"He must be in the rest room!"

Key West Recipes

Mike's Chewy Louie ♥ Heart Healthy Cookies

Ingredients	USA	Metric
Butter, Salted (Melted)	1 ½ Sticks	180 mL
Sweet Condensed Milk	7 Oz	200 mL
Sugar, Brown	½ Cup	120 mL
Flour, All Purpose	¼ Cup	60 mL
Oatmeal, Old Fashioned (Dry)	1 ½ Cup	360 mL
Coconut, Flakes	½ Cup	120 mL
Vanilla	1 Tbsp.	15 mL
Cinnamon	1 tsp	5 mL
Cranberries, Dried	1 Cup	240 mL
Clementine Peel, Finely Diced	1 Peel	20 mL

Chewy Louie "Heart ♥ Healthy" Oatmeal Cookies contain no eggs to reduce cholesterol and no added salt to help control blood pressure. The recipe will produce 72 small, flattened cookies that contain moderate amounts of fiber. Each cookie is only 52 calories to help control body weight.

In a large mixing bowl, add the following ingredients as indicated:

- Melted Butter
- Sweetened Condensed Milk

- Brown Sugar
- Flour
- Cinnamon
- Vanilla

Mix until a smooth and thick consistency is achieved.

Add the following remaining ingredients.

- Oatmeal, Old Fashioned (best not to use instant)
- Coconut Flakes or Shreds
- Diced Clementine or Orange Peel (very small)
- Dried Cranberries

Mix with a large spoon until all ingredients are well combined.

Using a teaspoon, position small amounts of dough on a quality baking sheet and place in a preheated 350° F (175° C) oven for 12 to 14 minutes. Remove from oven when the bottom of the cookies turn golden brown and allow the cookies to cool to room temperature. Store in a covered container. If cookies are too moist, bake again at 180° F (82°C) for 30 minutes for Crispy Chewy Louie Cookies!

Key Lime Pie Recipes

Included are two recipes for Key Lime Pie. The "original" version of Key Lime Pie made in Key West uses a regular pie crust and is topped with meringue. The second version is made with a graham cracker crust and is normally garnished with whipped cream and lime zest.

Original Key Lime Pie

Similar to a lemon meringue pie in appearance.

Pie Filling Ingredients	USA	Metric
Large Eggs	4	4
Sweet Condensed Milk	14 Oz	400 mL
Sugar, White	1/3 Cup	80 mL
Key Lime Juice	1/3 to 1/2 Cup	100 mL
Cream of Tartar	½ tsp	2.5 mL
Add Green Food Coloring if a greener pie appearance is desired		

Crust Directions:

Begin with an uncooked crust (home-made or purchased)

Place the crust in a pie pan and pierce the bottom crust with a fork to prevent bubbling. Many use pie weights so the crust will not bubble. Pinch the top edges of the crust before baking. Bake according to directions and allow to cool for 10 to 15 minutes prior to adding the filling.

Filling Directions:

Separate the egg yolks & egg whites into different glass bowls. After mixing the Sweetened Condensed Milk and Egg Yolks, gradually add the Key Lime Juice. Mix well and pour into the baked pie crust. Bake the filled pie for about 10 minutes at 350° (175° C) degrees. Allow to cool for 5-10 minutes.

Meringue Directions:

Whip the egg whites on high speed using a whisk attachment. Whisk until the egg whites create peaks. This will take 5-10 minutes. Slowly add Sugar and Cream of Tartar and whisk several more minutes.

Using a spatula, spoon the meringue on top of the pie. Be sure to spread the meringue out to the pie edges to limit shrinking as the pie cools. Bake pie & meringue at 350° degrees until meringue turns slightly brown. Continually observe the meringue while baking to prevent burning.

Remove the pie from the oven and allow to cool for about an hour. Refrigerate for several hours before serving.

New Key Lime Pie

Pie Filling Ingredients	USA	Metric
Large Eggs	3	3
Sweet Condensed Milk	14 Oz	400 mL
Lime Zest	1 tsp	5 mL
Key Lime Juice	2/3 Cup	200 mL

Crust Ingredients	USA	Metric
Graham Crackers	1/3 Lbs.	151 G
Melted Butter	5 Tbsp.	75 mL
Sugar, White	1/3 Cup	80 mL

Topping Ingredients	USA	Metric
Whipped Cream	To taste	To taste
Lime Slices	1 or 2	1 or 2
Lime Zest	To taste	To Taste

Graham Cracker Crust Directions:

Preheat oven to 350° (175° C)

Crush Graham Crackers with a rolling pin after inserting into a plastic bag or use a food processor. In a large bowl, combine the Crushed Graham Crackers, Melted Butter and Sugar. Stir until thoroughly combined and press into a pie pan forming a pie crust. Bake crust for 8 minutes and allow to cool on a wire rack.

Filling Directions:

After separating the Egg Yolks, beat one at a time with a mixer on high speed until the yolks become fluffy. This will take about 5 minutes. Slowly add the Sweetened Condensed Milk to the fluffy yolks and beat this mixture until thick. It may take about 4 minutes. Slow down the mixer speed and add the Key Lime Juice. Add Lime Zest into the mixture after setting a little aside to garnish. Do not overmix! Pour the pie filling into the waiting Graham Cracker Crust and pop the pie back into the 350° oven for about 10 minutes. Cool the pie on a rack and then refrigerate at least 15 minutes before serving. The pie can be garnished with Whipped Cream and Lime Slices.

Top with a little Lime Zest. Bon Appétit!

Black Bean Recipes

Cooking dried Black Beans is easy and tasty, but canned beans can be substituted and dressed up with the same spices as listed below.

Diane's Key West Black Beans

Ingredients	USA	Metric
Black Beans, Dried	1 Lb.	453 G
Water	8 Cups	1920 mL
Olive Oil	1 Tbsp.	15 mL
Salt	1 tsp	5 mL
Cumin	1 tsp	5 mL
Red Pepper	½ tsp	2.5 mL
Bay Leaves	3	3
Garlic Cloves	4	4
Onion, Medium	1	1
Optional Ingredients		
Black Beans, 15½ oz. Drained	3 Cans *	3 Cans *
Green Pepper, Diced	1	1
Lime Juice	To Taste	To Taste
Cilantro	To Taste	To Taste
Tomatoes, Diced, Small Can	14.5 oz.	411 G
Sazon Seasoning	1.41 oz.	40 G

(*) One pound of dried beans equals 5 to 6 cups cooked beans. One 15½-ounce can (drained) beans equals 1½ cups cooked beans. If a recipe calls for cooking 1 pound of dry beans, you could get the same amount of cooked beans from three 15½-ounce cans of drained beans.

Soaking Dried Black Beans will make them cook slightly faster. It is optional. I cook them in unsalted water and add seasoning later.

Cooking Directions:

Rinse Dried Black Beans in a colander removing any bad beans.

Place beans into a large pot with 8 cups of Water.

Add Onions and Garlic and Other Seasonings to the pot.

Cover the pot and bring the mixture to a boil, then lower the heat and stir often. Set a timer for an hour and then monitor until the beans are tender and plump. When tender and plump, add Bay Leaves, Cilantro, Lime Juice and Salt.

Black Beans may also be cooked in a crock pot for 3 to 4 hours. This does not have to be monitored as closely. You do not want to burn a pot of beans! A few burned beans will alter the entire pot of beans.

Serve with white or yellow rice.

Allow the remaining Black Beans to cool to room temperature before refrigerating. They will keep for approximately 4 or 5 days.

For a traditional and delicious Cuban meal serve Black Beans & Rice with either fish or Picadillo and Cuban Bread (substitute Baguette Bread).

Mike's Quick Black Beans

Ingredients	USA	Metric
Black Beans, 15½ oz. Drained	1 Can.	1 Can
Water	¾ Cup	240 mL
Olive Oil	¼ Cup.	180 mL
Salt	½ tsp	2.5 mL
Worcestershire Sauce	1 Tbsp.	15 mL
Liquid Smoke, Mesquite	2 tsp	10 mL

Cooking Directions:

Combine all ingredients in a medium pot and cook over medium heat until reaching a thick consistency. This usually requires ½ to ¾ of an hour. Intermittently stir to prevent burning at the bottom of the pot.

Serve over Rice or add to Tacos and Burritos for a tasty meal.

Cuban Picadillo Recipe

This is thought of as a Cuban Hash. It can be cooked with ground beef or ground pork. It is traditionally served over Black Beans & Rice. It can be made with or without potatoes and some folks omit the raisins. A dash of white wine will also add to the flavor.

Diane's Key West Picadillo

Ingredients	USA	Metric
Ground Beef or Pork	1 ½ Lb.	680 G
Large Potato, Cubed	1	1
Olive Oil	2 Tbsp.	30 mL
Salt	1 tsp	5 mL
Cumin	2 tsp	10 mL
Pepper, Black	½ tsp	2.5 mL
Red Sweet Pepper(Finely Diced)	1	1
Oregano	2 tsp	10 mL
Onion, Medium (Finely Diced)	1	1
Bay Leaves	2	2
Tomato Paste	1 Tbsp.	30 mL
Tomatoes, Diced	1 Cup	240 mL
Worcestershire Sauce	2 Tbsp.	30 mL
Pimento Green Olives	½ Cup	120 mL
Capers	2 Tbsp.	30 mL

Cooking Directions:

Heat Olive Oil in deep skillet. Add Meat and Sauté with Potato, Onion and Sweet Red Pepper until fully cooked. Add the remaining ingredients and cook for approximately 15 minutes. Serve hot over Black Beans & Rice or just over rice. Remove Bay Leaf pieces before serving.

Serve with white rice, black beans, and Cuban bread (substitute Baguette Bread).

Key West Fritters Recipe

Cuban Fritters (Bollitos)

Ingredients	USA	Metric
Black-Eyed Peas, Dried	1 Lb.	453 G
Bell Pepper, Diced	1	1
Onion, Medium, Diced	1	1
Salt	1 tsp	5 mL
Garlic Cloves, Minced	5	5
Red Bird Chili Peppers (Optional)	1 tsp	5 mL

Cooking Directions:

Soak the black-eyed peas in a gallon of water overnight.

Grind the peas in either coffee grinder or food processor.

Mix all ingredients until the batter is similar to cake batter.

Spoon the batter and form into a little ball (the size of a golf ball)

Heat 1 Cup of Sunflower or Canola Oil in a skillet.

Fry the Bollitos until golden in color. (Approximately 3 minutes)

Cooking Tips:

Do not place more than 4 or 5 Bollitos in the skillet at one time.

Drain after cooking on a paper towel and serve with sliced lime.

Diane's Conch Fritters

My first order of Conch Fritters came in a brown paper bag with a slice of lime. I have cooked these fritters for years, although it is hard to replicate eating them on a beach while looking out over the beautiful water and sky.

1. Heat sufficient oil in a deep pot to 350 degrees.
2. In a large bowl, combine Conch Meat, Bell Pepper, Garlic, Flour and Cornmeal as described below.
3. In a small bowl, whisk Milk and Egg together.
4. Combine all ingredients until they are well mixed into a batter.
5. Season this with Paprika, Salt and Cayenne Pepper.
6. Scoop balls of batter into the hot oil and cook 4 minutes or until golden brown. Drain thoroughly on paper towels and serve with lime.

Ingredients	USA	Metric
Conch Meat, Finely Chopped	1 Lb.	453 G
Bell Pepper, Finely Chopped	½ Cup	120 mL
Celery, Finely Chopped (Optional)	¼ Cup	60 mL
Flour	1 Cup	240 mL
Egg	1	1
Garlic Cloves, Minced	2	2
Cornmeal	3 tsp	15 mL
Milk	½ Cup	120 mL
Cayenne Pepper	¼ tsp	1 mL
Paprika	¼ tsp	1 mL
Salt	1 tsp	5 mL

Fried Plantains

Tostones

(Not Sweet Green Plantains)

These are served with traditional Cuban dishes like black beans & rice and *picadillo*. Plantains are a side dish served in preference to fried potatoes.

- Obtain Fresh Green Plantains: These will be green, firm and a knife may be needed to facilitate peeling. These are not black sweet plantains.
- Peel and slice the plantain into diagonal one-inch pieces.
- Fry the Plantains Pieces in a shallow frying pan under medium heat for approximately 5 minutes per side or until all sides are golden. (Avoid cooking too many plantain slices at a time)
- Verify that the pieces are thoroughly cooked before removing from the oil.
- Remove the pieces from the skillet and drain on paper towels to absorb the excess oil.
- Allow the fried pieces to cool a bit before starting the flattening process. Flatten the plantains with a piece of flat wood until 1/2 inch thick.
- Fry the flattened plantains for about 5 minutes in the same skillet, until crisp and golden on both sides. Remove and drain on paper towels.
- Season with salt.
- Serve with hot sauce, aioli or other sauces.
- Enjoy!

Maduros

(Sweet Black Plantains)

- Obtain Sweet Black Plantains: These are ripened plantains. The blacker they are, the sweeter they will be!
- Peel and slice into ¼ inch diagonal pieces. The thinner the pieces are, the crispier they will be!
- Fry the Plantains Pieces in a shallow frying pan under medium heat for approximately 2 minutes per side or until golden and crispy.
- Remove the Plantain Pieces from the skillet and drain on a paper towels to absorb the excess oil.
- Sprinkle with sugar and a little cinnamon to taste.
- Enjoy!

Diane Wheeler

Diane Wheeler was born in Pensacola, Florida in 1947 while her father was in flight training pursuing the "wings of gold." Florida was the first of many U.S. Navy ports that became her home and she attended many different elementary and junior high schools up and down the east coast. Her life changed forever when her family finally landed in Key West, Florida in 1961. No matter how many thousands of miles away she is, Diane has called Key West her home since the first glimpse of the little island.

Inspired to change the world one child at a time, she graduated from Illinois State University (Normal, IL) in 1975 with a BS in Elementary Education. In 2004 she received an MA in Multicultural Education from Florida Atlantic University. She has taught school over 30 years from Imperial County, California to Key West, Florida with multiple stops in between.

Diane enjoys watercolors, long hikes and camping trips, practices yoga and enjoys spending time with family. Since her very timid beginning, she has seldom met a person that remains a stranger.

Mike Kohut

Mike was born in Altoona, Pennsylvania in 1942 while his father, a Navy MD, served with the Marines in the Pacific during WWII. After the war, Mike's dad was assigned to Navy Hospitals across the US creating a gypsy lifestyle for the family.

Mike entered Key West High School in 1957 and graduated in 1961. After his father retired from the Navy, Mike's family relocated to State College, PA. Missing his paradise home, he returned to Key West in 1962 to start a new life on his own terms. Mike joined the Marine Corps in 1964, attended Electronics School in San Diego, CA. and graduated in 1965 as a Microwave Radio Technician. He then served with the 11th Marines in Viet Nam and was honorably discharged in 1968.

Graduating with a BS in Medical Microbiology in 1974, he trained as a Clinical Laboratory Scientist in 1975. Working with several technology companies, he combined his dual knowledge of electronics and medical technology in the medical instrumentation field.

Mike enjoys playing guitar and photographic art with his wife Kathie.

Acknowledgements

Writing a book is both a joyous and humbling experience. Behind our words and memories is a support group of family and friends who edited text, corrected grammar, checked punctuation, gifted photographs, formatted images and brought us together as coauthors. To this group of dedicated helpers we are forever thankful with sincere gratitude and admiration.

Editors:

Kathie Morrison Kohut
Denny Bast

Book Reviews:

Mary O'Neill
Yukiko Kitta

Photographic Contributions:

Nikki Pena-Infande
Karyn Morrison Nagel
Linda Lambert

Introductions:

Ruthie Watler Rivera

Key West Historians:

Bobby Pazo
Ray Gutierrez

CPSIA information can be obtained
at www.ICGtesting.com
Printed in the USA
LVHW072155030522
717903LV00032B/1083